The Challenge to Be and Not to Do

The Challenge to Be and Not to Do

How to Manage Your Career and Maximize Your Potential

Carrie Foster

BEP BUSINESS EXPERT PRESS

The Challenge to Be and Not to Do: How to Manage Your Career and Maximize Your Potential
Copyright © Business Expert Press, LLC, 2018.

First published in 2018 by
Business Expert Press, LLC
222 East 46th Street, New York, NY 10017
www.businessexpertpress.com

ISBN-13: 978-1-63157-774-1 (paperback)
ISBN-13: 978-1-63157-775-8 (e-book)

Business Expert Press Human Resource Management and Organizational Behavior Collection

Collection ISSN: 1946-5637 (print)
Collection ISSN: 1946-5645 (electronic)

Cover and interior design by S4Carlisle Publishing Services
Private Ltd., Chennai, India

First edition: 2018

10 9 8 7 6 5 4 3 2 1

Printed in the United States of America.

Abstract

This book, promotes the idea that every individual has a unique talent potential. It aims to encourage individuals to seek out their talent and release their potential. Essentially, it challenges us all to be defined by who we are, not what we do.

Keywords

Attitude to Aptitude, Being not Doing, Career Development, People First, Talent Development

Contents

Preface

I have the privilege of working with adult learners in a number of capacities. Whether it is working as a lecturer at a university, coaching or working with teams, departments, or whole organizations in my role as an organization development practitioner, the same lack of confidence in talent and our unique self is universal. Even the seemingly most self-absorbed individuals who apparently appear oblivious to their weaknesses are filled with the most crushing aspects of self-doubt.

I stand in front of leadership groups exhorting them to BE the best leader they can be and I get worried looks and gallows humor. To stand in front of a group of individuals in corporate life and declare that I am awesome—I am by the way—is met with suspicion and an uncomfortable shift in their seats.

At what point do we stop believing that we CAN be and do anything that we set our minds to? In part, the blame lives in the education system, which measures everyone by the same yard stick of academic ability, rather than seek to realize the unique ability and talent (whatever that is) of each individual. But, it is also part of our cultural, social, economic, and political makeup. The discomfort we feel at someone saying they are awesome is programmed into us. Thou Shalt Not Boast.

This book is written with a heartfelt belief that YOU ARE awesome and YOU do have a unique talent. This exhortation isn't just for your benefit; it is for all our benefits.

Our deepest fear is not that we are inadequate. Our deepest fear is that we are powerful beyond measure. It is our light, not our darkness that most frightens us. We ask ourselves, who am I to be brilliant, gorgeous, talented, fabulous? Actually, who are you not to be? You are a child of God. You playing small does not serve the world. There is nothing enlightened about shrinking so that other people won't feel insecure around you. We are all meant to shine, as children do. We were born to make manifest the glory of God that is within us. It's not just in some of us; it's in everyone. And as we let our own light shine, we unconsciously give other people permission to do the same. As we are liberated from our own fear, our presence automatically liberates others.

—Marianne Williamson

Acknowledgment

This book reflects a personal journey of discovering who I am, who I am meant to be rather than do. I would like to thank my friends and family who have supported me through my own journey of discovery, especially my best friend and husband who has held me up and encouraged me to find out what my true calling is. I would like to thank all my clients who have allowed me to practice being in their organizations and my colleagues who have accepted my candor in difficult times. I would like to thank BEP for giving me the opportunity to write what I am passionate about and for providing me with a platform from which I can share my mission to release the talent potential in everyone.

Introduction

It's Time to Reclaim Our
Right to Be Human

The strongest force in the universe is a human being living consistently with his identity.

—Tony Robbins

I'd like to blame industrialization for the problems we see in our struggle to be human. The modern workplace began with the clunk, clack of the machines of our Victorian brethren. First, there was the development of noisy, smelly steam engines and factories, which destroyed the livelihood of the artisans and then there was the push for efficiency through design. Taylor (1911) bought us 'scientific management' but this was just the beginning of a cacophony of management approaches that have scourged the workplace focused on the machinations of what we do and how efficiently we do things. However, in truth, the human, the 'who we are', was lost long before Stephenson's Rocket (1826) puffed its way into the history book. The very origin of our names: Smith, Potter, Cooper, Mason, Taylor, Tyler, Baker, and Spicer—are all based on occupations, on what we do. It seems it is part of the human condition to label and categorize people by what we see them doing, rather than enjoying understanding who they are. Part of that is ease and speed. Labels help us to categorize and make sense of the world that we live in. It is true the Victorians went a little bit overboard, categorizing and measuring everything in the drive for modernity and scientific understanding, but it has to be said that it's difficult to label what makes someone . . . them. Your job title isn't who you are. It corresponds to some activity that you do that you get paid for, but even then the label doesn't exactly sum you up neatly because there's all this other stuff that you do that lies on the edges or outside of the box that a job title places you in.

Take being a parent for instance. Very often, a 'stay-at-home mom or dad' is reduced to 'looks after the kids', but whether intended to be funny or a serious pushback against this demeaning of their role in society, stay-at-home parents will fight back with a list of job titles that looking after the kids involves citing everything from housekeeper to finance director, to search and rescue, particularly for lost toys. However, despite the large number of jobs a mom or dad does, even these titles do not encompass who that person really is. Many parents decry their loss of self in the midst of diapers and school runs, feeling that they can't be who they are when all their energy is focused on wiping little Johnny's snot from his nose. In part, this is because what we do, our jobs, are an extension of who we are.

In many ways, our work helps us to define self. Maslow (1962) used the term 'self-actualization' to describe the point at which we become self-fulfilled and our jobs help us do that. Not everyone has the privilege of working in a profession or workplace that is fulfilling, and I would argue that the loss of self extends beyond the struggles of a stay-at-home mom or dad to all those who lose who they are in a job that sucks the life out of them. For too many, the dream job or the goal to work somewhere, doing something that is meaningful remains out of reach. It is in many ways, the point of this book, to challenge you to find an occupation that helps you to BE you and not settle for just doing a job. This shouldn't be the preserve of the rich or the lucky few. It has to be a determined resistance against accepting second best and a false presumption that there is nothing better for you.

The Challenge to BE in the Modern World

In a technologically driven global economy, everything is digitalized. Hundreds of thousands of gigabytes of data are reduced to a series of 0 and 1 sequences and transferred across the ether every second of everyday. We now live in the networked society, where our lives are played out, not just in the streets where we live and work, but in a virtual world where our identity is tied to the number of followers and likes we have.

This revolution has occurred quickly; the first desktop computers only became available in the mid1970s, broadband internet arrived in 2000, and 3G making mobile access possible in 2001. Social networking began in 2003 with MySpace and, within a decade, we were more connected and networked than ever before. It has transformed work, not just in how we do it, but what work we do and it has transformed the way we live our lives. We are now encouraged to build our online footprint, share our information, and contribute content to be found, seen, and heard. If we get notice, we go viral. It's no longer just about our qualification to do a job or our skills at least in the traditional sense. Those with a talent to entertain, pull epic pranks, or just pull together great cat memes can all be recognized and lauded. Putting faces to names is no longer a problem. We can Google anyone and chances are, in less time than it takes to order a Skinny White and armed only with a name and small amount of details, we are likely to find a picture of anyone, a detailed profile, and numerous thoughts and ideas that they have shared with the world.

However, the way we engage with the virtual world is completely different from the way we live in the real world. We present a public relations version of reality. The virtual reality is not the same as reality, reality. Celebrity news reports suggest that Kim Kardashian took several thousand selfies on a four-day vacation to Mexico, but only spent four hours on the beach. That's not a holiday; that's work. It also begs the question as to how many photos that made the grade were filtered, cropped, and touched up to be uploaded, a presentation of a fake reality. So, when we read the job titles people give themselves on social media platforms, it is not like a job title you are given to denote a job you do. Unlike the real world where the job title we are given is based upon the context of our position within an organization in recognition of our ranking within an industry, we can label ourselves anything we like. We can call ourselves expert or declare ourselves an authority in anything, merely by adding the tag 'expert' to our profile. There is no qualification to being an expert, no bar that has to be reached that separates an expert from a no-expert. You simply have to know, or be good at pretending to know, more than someone else. This development of fakery isn't a new phenomenon; people have postured and posed as professionals from the moment that doing so gave them an economic and social advantage. I'm also fairly convinced that for many of those who have a title or have earned the professional prefix probably spend a greater amount of time worrying that they are going to be 'found out' as not really knowing what they are talking than the rest of worry about achieving that level of recognition. In many ways, the acquiring of titles and recognition is the biggest game of charades that has ever been played by society.

However, what is clear is that web 2.0 enables us to fabricate and construct a false reality, than say, someone writing a book, who can only become an expert if their expertise is recognized as such by those people who have read the book. In fact lies and fake news is such a problem, it's become a thing in its own right. You can choose to avoid taking things at face value and take time to research, find out, and investigate to find the truth. But what if the truth, online at least, is manufactured? What if, the information you are reading has been planted, created, and tested to ensure that what you are reading, though not true, is endorsed by those we trust, paid for, and manipulated to such an extent that it becomes truth.

This is no small thing, because job titles and professional expertise represent something culturally. It has meaning and importance. The labels we use to describe a person's worth, they give or take away authority and with that our power to get things done. From an early age, we are conditioned to understand the difference a title makes to our position in society and the way we are treated if we are the one with the title. In the UK, we have hereditary titles such as Her/His Majesty (HM) used by the Queen and HRH, Her/His Right Honorable, holders of which are children of HM, and hold that title by accident of birth. We also have a chivalric honor system, which bestows titles on people for their services to the arts and sciences, charitable works, and public service. This system confers the title of Sir and Dame and rewards the holder with a position of knighthood, though, I presume without the horse and armor. Professions also exclude those who are not part of the club through the use of monikers, whether it is Doctor, Professor, Chartered etc. or postnominal titles. The title or letters after your name are given as recognition of professional competence and qualification, and with it, bestow an expectation of expertise. These titles exist because they matter. They confer an importance; a cut above others, and the same is true in corporate life. President, Vice President, Chief Executive Officer, Director; they all give prestige and privilege. It is, therefore, not a surprise that we adapt our titles online to make us sound more important, more qualified, and more worthy of respect.

Comparing Ourselves to Others

There are many things about the world we live in that are good and provide exciting opportunities, but there are also many things that bring darkness and reduce our humanity. One of the most disturbing aspects about social media is the increase in superficial comparison. Who we are has become less important than the image we project and our outward appearance of success. Mental illness is rising with 24 percent of adults suffering from mental health conditions such as anxiety or depression (NHS Digital, 2014). In part, this is driven by our need to compare our mundane ordinary lives to the perfect more glamorous life portrayed by others on social media. Although portraying ourselves in pictures is not new, Hans Holbein (1497–1593) wouldn't have had a career if he couldn't paint portraits for Northern European royalty and the wealthy aristocracy, it's primacy as a form of self-expression is. The combination of social media accounts and the technology offered by front-facing cameras on the iPhone 4 in 2010 spawned the modern selfie trend (Losse, 2013).

Today, selfies are part of the online marketing of self. The mass population now has an opportunity to explore portraiture without the need of an accomplished and expensive artist. A mode of self-expression, it is used to provide a sense of self, while, at the same time, providing a record of self-observation. But, due to the ability to take as many selfies as necessary to get the best angle, light, and deliver that killer photograph, the selfie we upload is actually an expression about who we desire to be.

The obsession with self-image, or rather the doctoring of selfie images, means that our understanding of self is being eroded. For some, this is simply narcissism, placing us, quite literally, at the center of the world in which we live. For others, there is a sense that selfies have taken on a life of their own, which has meant that they normalize idealized perfection and posturing, while stripping away authenticity. Filters and photo manipulation tools means that we can banish wrinkles, reduce waist sizes, and enhance assets in ways that even the most flattering of portrait artists would have been embarrassed to succumb to. This, in turn, has led to an increase in plastic surgery among young people as they seek surgical fixes to perceived imperfections. According to the American Society of Plastic Surgery, 15.9 million cosmetic surgery procedures were performed in the

US in 2015, a rise of 115 percent since 2000 (ASPS, 2016). The result is that many young people look like clones or previously natural beauties have gone under the knife to emerge with an esthetically pleasing version of themselves, which, all the same, doesn't quite look right. However, in the UK, there seems to be a backlash, with cosmetic surgery levels falling by 40 percent in 2016 (Grierson, 2017). Apparently this phenomenon is due to an increase in 'real' social media celebrities. Which even when typing the sentence reeks of absurdity. REAL social media celebrities are not real. They are not the person you see when the Youtube video ends. They are the edited version of a virtual reality that has a tenuous connection to the person they are when not under self-imposed scrutiny.

Our lives are being documented in ways that could never have been imagined by the diarists of yesteryear. Everything we do is recorded in full Technicolor glory, and that means we have to be more than ordinary. It's like a permanent competition to seem interesting. My daughter's school sends home the class cuddly toy for the weekend with one of the children. If you read through the adventures of the stuff toy it would appear that every member of my daughter's class has a fabulously amazing weekend of fun activities and adventures every weekend. Ever the subversive, I refused to change our plans from 'pajama day' and a 'family film time' after a particularly busy and tiring week working in the Middle East; glamorous, international businesswoman Monday to Friday, knackered mother who needs a lie in at the weekend. The pressure to perform is ridiculous, and this is an exercise book sent home by primary school teachers for 'fun'. This psychology of attraction goes beyond simply trying to develop romantic attachment, it is linked to an interpersonal judgment (Byrne, 1961) that is the bread and butter of our social interactions. Status and health are the foundations of our social standing and acceptance. It is, therefore, unsurprising that our social media 'status' becomes an unending competition to do something interesting.

It is no longer possible to simply enjoy cheese on toast. Every meal has to look like a gourmet dinner so we can insta or snapchat a picture of our food intake. The way we look has become more important as we are judged on the selfies we post, there are increasing levels of eating disorders as young people engage in an unending pursuit of physical perfection to compete and people get into debt trying to buy into the last status symbols. It's an exhausting and permanent cycle of being on display. The Internet is the modern day Versailles, a mirage of sumptuous ceremony and a living tableaux of human vanity. We ignore the reality of unfulfilling lives and instead feed ourselves on fake news, choosing to spend our time living in our social media bubbles to insulate us from the truth.

More than Just a Number

As we grow up, we have become used to being attributed numbers. Social security number, employee number, driver's license number, passport number, bank account number; in the UK, we have NHS numbers, NI numbers, council tax references, and every item or service that you buy is attributed a contract number. We end up with so many numbers it is impossible to keep them all in our heads, so whenever we ring up a service we have to have the number to hand because they can't find 'us' if we don't have a number.

The systems we have to navigate in the modern world to organize our lives throw up many ridiculous scenarios. I have been in a bank lobby where a regular customer, who the counter staff welcomed by name, couldn't draw money out of her account because she didn't have her card, or her account number. The staff couldn't provide her with the account number because she didn't have proof of who she was, even though they knew who she was. Or take the example of my husband who received a phone call from a service provider to his mobile phone, but because he 'failed' the security question and didn't have his account number to hand they couldn't discuss his account with him, even though they were the ones who rang him. In regards to life online, in 2012, Philip Roth was forced to write an open letter to Wikipedia in the New Yorker because he was unable to get a correction about his own novel posted on the Wikipedia page because he, the author of the book, was not a credible source. Only after the open letter was published, did Wikipedia allow the correction to be made. The mind boggles as to how machines, rules, and the processes we submit our lives to have managed to become so dictatorial that human intervention is no longer considered a valid reason to question the outcome, but here we are. "Computer says no" is funny because we have all experience being prevented in being able to do something, because of a machine.

The real tragedy in all of this is that we have allowed ourselves to be stripped of who we are. It is no wonder that many fall into despair and depression when individuals are faced with a world where no one connects with them on an authentic level. Our transactions and activities on the Web are monitored by algorithms, which attribute categories to us and label us for marketing in order to sell us more goods and services. We are no longer human beings who think, feel, and exist; we are data to be exploited and used for nefarious purposes.

But, it is not just faceless corporations who assign us to a category. We tag ourselves with labels "I am a [job title/race/gender/sexual orientation etc.]" but in the midst of all this labeling, tagging, and numbering, we forget who we really are, losing ourselves in the process. We are so busy trying to describe what we do, we don't have the time to explore who we are, what our potential talent could lead us to be. In education, our quirks are beaten out of us, and we learn to conform to norms and standards of behavior, which are deemed socially acceptable. Like machines, we are expected to get 'with the program' and keep inside the lines, instead of pursuing a purpose that is decidedly multicolored and refuses to be restricted by the norms and expectations of others. In a society, which offers a world of opportunity and possibility, we are becoming more homogenized and alike than we would care to admit. I look at young women on the train and their faces, thick with makeup, have lost their personal quirks in a pursuit for standardized perfection. Even CVs which should be something that should be something, that is, as individual as we are all, begin to read alike; excellent communication skills, goal orientated, motivated, strong work ethic. In our pursuit of standing out from the crowd, our actions result in bland replication and sameness. These are the CVs that make me want to scream "who are you?" The real you, not the social media selfie, or twenty tips for getting your next job standardized profile. If we were to strip away the onion layers of frippery and fakery, what is left? That's the challenge to BE.

Stop thinking about how to present yourself to common standards and begin to embrace how unique and wonderful you are. Rather than losing track of the talent you have, pursue an awakening of self-awareness. Stop allowing yourself to be shuttled into doing a job you hate, for money that you can barely survive on. We must stop calling ourselves successful if we have money at the end of the month when we no longer know why we are doing what we are doing. If we don't have any purpose to our lives other than to reaching the next pay check, then we are not reaching our full potential; we are existing and we deserve more than to just simply exist.

We have stopped being, and we are doing lots of stuff, some of it really good, but none of it connecting us to who we are and what we should be doing. We have become victims of imprisonment and haven't even noticed that we have lost our freedom to be who we are supposed to be. You might remember the moment you gave up dreaming, dismissing you hopes as if they were childlike toys that needed to be packed away along with your Action Men and Barbie Dolls, but we have a lot to learn from children in re-establishing a belief that we CAN BE something amazing, unique, and wonderful. In fact, we already are.

It's time to stop. You are more than a social media profile can ever show. You are more than a number or username that resides in an impenetrable system. It's time to reclaim who you are. It's time to stop doing and start being. The challenge to Be and not to Do requires you to put aside your doubts and past hurts, to realize that you can determine the path you take and that the thoughts and dreams that we hold close are a reflection of who we are.

Manage Your Career Tool #1 – Your Personal Brand Profile

This tool is one that I developed over a number of years, which is based upon principles of product brand design. It may seem strange, having exhorted you to become more human, to use a tool that has its beginnings in products and services. However, the whole point of brand development in marketing is to help describe and develop a brand that gives the product human traits and characteristics. The marketing industry uses Aristotle's ingredients for persuasion; ethos, pathos, and logos to imbue products with credibility and character, create an emotional response in consumers, and use reason to persuade us to buy in the promise. At the same time, ironically, the recruitment industry has been removing these elements from CVs to professionalize them, aka. Turning us all into robots.

The tool uses the psychology of randomization to burrow into your subconscious and force you to reveal a little a bit about who your really are. Some people working through this tool may find it simple to use, others a painful endeavor. Whatever your experience, I encourage you to work through it diligently, and not shy away from words that might make you feel uncomfortable or vulnerable. The aim is help you to articulate who you really are and that shouldn't be edited out.

There are four tasks to complete:

Task 1 – What are you?
Task 2 – Meet. . .
Task 3 – A profile for. . .
Task 4 – Who are you?

Do not second-guess yourself and trust in the process. The end result should be a true reflection of who you really are, capturing your true character, and appealing to the reader on an emotional and rational level. Be honest and truthful in completing this task and the end result will be a powerful statement, which you can use as a professional profile on your resume or curriculum vitae.

Task 1 – What Are You?

Complete the table below answering the question:

If you were a (see list below) what would you be and Why?
Example: Color Red – I am Bright, Vibrant, Passionate

Object	What	Why
Example Sound	*Rushing waterfall*	*I am energetic, I like to carve out niche(s) for myself and choose my own way, go with the flow*
Sound		
Musical Instrument		
Country		
Plant		
Color		
Object		
Building		
Perfume /Aftershave		
Food Dish		

Task 2 – Meet. . .

Transfer the things that you have put in the 'WHAT' column in Task 1 into the table below. Describe each of these 'things' as if they were a person. Tell me about their personality, characteristics, behaviour, attitudes etc. Write as if you were introducing him or her to me and you were providing a brief profile.

What	Meet (What) He/She is. . . .
Example Country Switzerland	*A meticulous timekeeper, very organized when it matters, likes processes that work, but pragmatic enough to focus more on the big picture and what can be achieved now. Celebrates beauty and creativity.*
Sound	
Musical Instrument	
Country	
Plant	
Color	
Object	
Building	
Perfume /Aftershave	
Food Dish	

Task 3 – A Profile for. . .

Write a Profile for a person, at least 8 sentences long, which use the words or phrases in the Why and Meet (What) column in Tasks 1 and 2. Just to be clear. You are writing this profile for a person who you are introducing to someone else (if it helps, think about writing a profile for this person for one of your clients). But use the 'words' and 'phrases' you've already written—even if the language may be something you would normally shy away from using.

This Person is _____

_____

_____

_____

_____

_____

_____

_____

_____

_____

Task 4 – Who Are You?

Rewrite and Polish Task 3, but start the profile with [Your Name]. Do not change words or phrases to something that you haven't used in the previous tasks, but do make sure it makes sense for you.

_____

_____

_____

_____

_____

_____

_____

_____

_____

_____

_____

_____

_____

_____

_____

_____

CHAPTER 1

Putting People First

Our inventions are wont to be pretty toys, which distract our attention from serious things. They are but improved means to an unimproved end.
—Henry David Thoreau

I have recently finished writing another book, which examines the role of capitalism and human capital in our economic life. Whilst researching for the project, I was struck by the way in which the capitalist system is based on the notion of 'price' while being associated ideologically with freedom. The conclusion I came to during my research was that capitalism really does place a price on freedom and it is a lot higher than you might think. For too many of us, we spend our lives in servitude to others. Whether it is our corporate masters, our creditors, or simply the system in which we live, we have a veneer of freedom, but are restricted into selling our labor to people who charge a very high rent on our productivity. I realize this makes me sound like a Marxist. I'm not, I'm a Temperatist, but the point I'm making is that the system in which we operate means we have an illusion of freedom and we have a price on our heads.

In organizational life, our value to an organization is also based on price. Our ability to get a job, and get paid a salary that reflects our worth is based on the market economy. If the markets says sports stars are worth millions and nurses mere thousands, then that dictates how much a health care professional will get paid regardless of the number of lives they save, or indeed the value of saving the life of the millionaire sports star. How much we are paid and how much we cost the company to employ us is recorded in minute detail on workforce spreadsheets and on an outgoing line on the profit and loss (P&L) account. Just think about that for a minute, the marvelous complexity of a human being with all their potential, knowledge, skills, and talent boiled down to a number on a spreadsheet. Your life reduced to dollars and cents.

The problem with a person being reduced to a number on a spreadsheet is that when an organization is faced with cost cutting due to economic pressures, leadership teams and accountants scour the ledgers to see where a reduction can be made in cost. Inevitably, they come to rest on the cost of human capital, one of the biggest variable costs that an organization will have, but the number itself hides all the complexities of human interaction within the organization. A simple calculation will be made of what cost needs to be trimmed, a number will be determined, a line is put through the head count figure, and the conversation moves on to other cost savings, marketing budgets, training budgets, capital equipment, stockholding etc. It may be that the process is less mechanical than that and some manager will take care to avoid delayering and redundancies, but many seasoned senior managers will have become hardened to the realities of the process and accept the inevitability of the process. They may not relish the uncertainty, unless of course the organizational restructure will be an opportunity to get rid of the deadwood in the organization.

The nefarious process of business re-engineering then filters down the organizational structure like slow moving volcanic lava, catching fire and bringing heat wherever it sets its path. Senior managers will instruct middle managers as to what their new revised budget for headcount will be and are told to get on with it, possibly with some support from Human Resources. The managers then get on with managing the impossible, carrying on with business as usual while seeing a reduction in productivity as the change program forced upon them demotivates staff. On their own, or with others, the manager will pull together a restructure plan to decide how to reduce the headcount while still being able to get the same amount of work done without any detriment to customer service and quality, and a redundancy program begins.

A simple line on a P&L sheet, collateral damage, and lives are boiled down to a number.

Inevitably, what happens is a few months down the line, when the dust has settled, the senior management team are tearing the hair out because someone vital to the smooth running of the organization, the person with the know-how to solve that particular problem has gone. The result is that all that intrinsic knowledge, specialist skills, human touch went walking out the door with their redundancy notice in hand. Ex-colleagues become consultants who charge more for the same work they were doing for less as an employee and before long there is a recruitment drive after another senior management team meeting where it is decided that a new division or project team is required. This time the number on the spreadsheet is crossed out and made bigger and the middle managers are required to spend time creating job specifications, interviewing for key strategic positions, and inducting new employees. And so the numbers game continues, up and down, down and up, and all the while people, with hopes and dream, bills to pay, kids to feed are added or subtracted in line with the vague notion of business performance.

The Misuse of Statistics on an International Level

In geo-political terms, this process of humans as numbers plays out as government statistics and blaring headlines in the media. In the last ten years, the scale of human tragedy reduced to numbers has, I believe numbed us to what the reality really is. Following the fall out of the 2008 credit crunch, the Greek government debt crisis caused a storm to erupt among members of the European Union. Hundreds of families have been forced to abandon their children because they can no longer afford to look after them and unemployment is running at 23.5 percent, double the Eurozone average. For the Greek youth, unemployment is running at 47.9 percent (Trading Economics, 2017), while the European Union insists on austerity measures and reforms in return for a bailout.

Perhaps the greatest tragedy, in regards to the human toll, at the time of writing this book is that of the civil war in Syria. Since the Arab Spring in 2011, more than eleven million Syrians have been killed or forced to leave their homes. There are 4.8 million Syrians who have sought safety in neighboring countries, making them the largest refugee population in the world, while 6.3 million are displaced within Syria itself. These numbers represent half of the population of Syria before the war began. Of the 2.5 million child refugees, 50 percent have lost everything; family, their home, their school, and their friends (Mercy Corps, 2017). Whether it is the need to find shelter, food, or being kept safe from human traffickers and exploitation, a whole generation of the Syrian child is being left to fend for themselves.

I doubt that a single person will look at these figures and not think that this situation is awful, and yet in the West we argue about immigration figures, the number of nondomestic nationals that should be allowed into the country, and the perceived threat to our way of life if we let these people in. There is a genuine and real concern about the possible terrorist threats posed by the Islamic State of Iraq and Syria (ISIS). However, because ISIS operates in Syria, there is an assumption that the refugees are Islamist extremists and that Muslims are a threat to our country. During the Second World War, 60 million people were displaced because of the War, including 12 million Germans. Syria is the second-largest migrant crisis in human history. Fear means that instead of extending a helping hand, we are erecting barriers and check points. To put the international response to the Syria crisis in context, the 1983–1984 Ethiopian famine killed 400,000–500,000 people (de Waal, 1991). The international community bought millions of records of two charity singles, one recorded by Band Aid and the other US for Africa and the Live Aid even raised £145 million.

The crisis in Syria has been met with disdain and suspicion, and yet these are people, just like you and me, with hopes, dreams, and desires. For many, they have gone from a life where they were getting up, going to work, and worrying about the kind of things you and I worry about, to fleeing for their lives, uncertain of where the next meal will come from, and scared for their family and friends. The politicians and the policy makers reduce these people to a number of immigrants that need to be controlled. They devalue their very humanity by recording them as a number on a spreadsheet, a statistic to be discussed around a boardroom table. Many spreadsheets have columns that report larger numbers as data ranges to remove zeros. That removes the person. Their skills, knowledge, and abilities are ignored, and their potential is reduced to a number.

What the world measures and determines as being really important is the wrong way round and yet every day we continue to take part in a system, making decisions that 'devalue' people to a number.

The Value of People in an Organization

In corporate life, this anachronism is played out daily. Ask a manager what an extra day's holiday is going to cost the business and he'll reel off a number. Ask him what value spending time with family and friends has to his workers and you'll get a blank stare and possibly a response about "What has that got to do with the price of eggs?" If I were to ask you to find out the cost of training in your organization, it would be a simple case of looking in the right ledger. If I were to ask you to find out the value of human potential and talent in your organization, the answer would be impossible to find. We simply do not have the ability to create a metric, which will provide a measure of a person's potential and value. Instead, we focus on what we can measure, which is cost. The reasons for this are simple. Human potential is subjective, and even to the human whose potential is being examined, unknown. We might know what you are capable of now, because of what you are able to demonstrate in terms of skill, knowledge, and ability, but we cannot know for certainty whether you have reached the limit of your potential or whether we are just glimpsing a small proportion of something truly marvelous.

The problem is of course that we don't recognize that people have potential that might have a value. If I were to ask you to give me a value of your capital equipment—then you could tell me the cost and the benefit associated with the plant in your business. What is more, you'll be able to tell me the utilization of the capital equipment, how much of its potential you are actually tapping into. So we do value potential, just not that of people. The end result is that people are reduced to a resource in a machine, a cog in a wheel, and in this reductionism, we lose something that makes people more valuable than capital equipment, or acceptable statistics and results. We lose a contribution that can only be found in humans. Creativity, innovation, collaboration, and that something that enables us as a species to develop beyond what our ancestors thought was humanly possible. What makes us fantastic is all the stuff that can't be measured, that precludes us from being in the box that stops us being like others. It is the quirks, the unique traits, the off-kilter thinking and the singular, one of the kind-ness that reaches beyond a skill that can be learned, knowledge that can be experienced or abilities that can be developed.

I want to challenge you to adopt a different perspective, just for a few hours to begin with. I want you to observe people, look around your organization, and ask yourself not what the people are costing the business, but what value they are adding. Conduct a thought experiment whereby you ponder what value they could add to the organization that, to date they have not yet been provided with the opportunity to release. You'll find that your P&L account is missing an important line in assets—people potential value or PPV for those who like three-letter acronyms. The next steps are obvious;

- What would it take to release the full potential of individuals within your organization?
- What opportunities do you need to create to make that happen?
- What conversations need to be had with managers and with individuals to make room for releasing potential
- What role and responsibilities do you have to make that a reality?
- What responsibility does the individual have in making the most of that opportunity?
- When are you going start?

We all need to step away from the salary we are paid and stop measuring ourselves by the number that the market, corporation, or government gives to us. We need to start thinking about the value that we can all add in regards to our very own performance potential. Challenging others and ourselves to think outside of the managerial constraints of easy metrics requires that we adopt a new attitude, which puts people first. Adopting this attitude will lead to a discovery that you can deliver a value far greater than the number you have been allocated. The change that is required is that you must be prepared to be more than what you do.

You need to be ready to act as if you are a value-adding asset beyond the market rate that forces you allow to be merely a cost to the organization. It's time that price was replaced by value in our economic system and people rather than capital were given priority.

Manage Your Career Tool #2 – Focus on Your Strengths

Adapted from (Buckingham, 2010)

In my early career as a People and Organization Development practitioner, I read a book by Marcus Buckingham called "Now discover your strengths" and it was a revelation. The basic premise of the book is that we need to identify our strengths and we will be more productive if we develop our strengths rather than focusing on correcting our weak areas. Today, it is perhaps one of my greatest frustrations with people development processes in organizations that there is an insistence on focusing on people's weaknesses that need fixing when it comes to people development planning. Why do that? If an organization invested its capital resources in stuff it was rubbish at, then it is obvious to anyone that it wouldn't take very long for the business to be out of business. I, therefore, cannot understand why this practice is the approach taken when it comes to identifying learning and development needs. Therefore, when it comes to your own personal development, there are two rules:

1. Focus on your strengths. At least 80 percent of your personal development plan should be focused on developing stuff you are really good at, to make you even better at doing them.
2. Only develop your weaknesses so far as they don't get in the way of you playing your strengths, but realize that overplaying strengths can make them into weaknesses. So develop a self-awareness of when that happens.

Identifying strengths is probably the hardest thing we need to do, partly because, if we are working within an area of strength, we will feel like we are in a natural flow and, therefore, we don't notice that it is something we are good at. Being able to do something without difficulty is usually an area in which you have a talent but we don't see it as a talent, because we can just do it. Get feedback from others and notice the things that you can do that you can't explain how you do them. You can just . . .

do them. These are possible areas of talent potential. The next step is to articulate your strengths. There are 3 tasks to do this:

1. Log activities
2. Articulate strengths
3. Write a strengths statement

Writing strengths statements can seem a bit laborious, but it is important that you do this exercise on a regular basis. Changing context and circumstances mean that we have an opportunity to discover more strengths that we did not know we had. For example, I didn't know I had a strength as a facilitator until I was moved on to a project at work, which gave me that opportunity. The end result was I loved the satisfaction that developing people gave me, that I changed career.

Task 1 – Log Activities

Over the course of a week, log any work tasks and activities that you have been involved in. Concentrate on activities and tasks that you do yourself. Think about how it felt when you were doing the tasks. Consider whether the task was one that enjoyed doing (liked), or one that you perhaps procrastinated about, and tried to avoid (disliked).

Liked	Disliked
For example – wrote an article for a journal	*For example – created tutor resources*

Task 2 – Articulate Strengths

Having identified those activities that you liked, consider how it is those activities make you feel effective. Rewrite the tasks listed in the liked column to make it identifiable as strength

For example, I feel strong when I write.

_____

_____

_____

_____

_____

_____

_____

_____

_____

_____

_____

_____

_____

_____

Task 3 – Write a 'strengths statement'

Buckingham (2010) states that you can "write a strengths statement by taking the verb (the doing word) and then drill down into what context you feel most strong in."

For example, I feel strong when writing about ideas that I have in areas in which I am knowledgeable and are connected to my passion for releasing people potential.

_____

_____

_____

_____

_____

_____

_____

_____

_____

_____

_____

_____

_____

_____

_____

_____

_____

CHAPTER 2

2 + 2 = 4

The whole is greater than the sum of its parts.

—Aristotle

Some days, I feel exasperated when talking to Senior Business Leaders who all nod their heads when you explain about people being an asset that harnesses competitive advantage and adds value. I watch them nodding their heads, but know that really they're agreeing politely while shaking their subconscious head, thinking, "Yes I know this is important but . . ." In the complex world of a dynamic and global economy, and the focus on fast capitalism with quarterly returns, there is little room for organizational leaders to focus on people things. They have to hit financial targets or face losing shareholder confidence. The bar is set high. Organizations need to demonstrate that they are growing fast, that costs are under control, and the business is lean and efficient. Leaders need to be decisive and have a plan that they are delivering against now, if not yesterday. There is no room for long-term thinking, investment in soft stuff, and going the extra mile to engage people, unless there is demonstrable return on investment (ROI) from the activity before the year end.

Try telling an organizational leader that their short-term thinking is going to result in long-term problems. That a short cut, which will lead to a celebrated profit made today, is creating a root that will eventually bring down the house of cards. Some of the smoke and mirrors that are used by organizations to make their balance sheet look healthy make the mind boggle. Whether it is divesting of buildings and renting them back or letting go of permanent staff to employ them as contractors, the fixed cost versus variable cost machinations would confuse even the most business savvy individual. Consider if you will the collapse of the subprime market in 2008. Finance houses and banks had been making significant profit returns right up to the credit crunch. Lehmann brother reported billion-dollar profits year-on-year from 2005 to 2007. In 2007, it communicated record net income and revenue results to its shareholders and yet on 15th September 2008, it filed for bankruptcy, the largest in history. Its collapse precipitated a global financial crisis and, ten years on, the effects of the credit crunch and the resulting sovereign debt crisis mean that austerity, wage stagnation, and unemployment are every day realities, and yet for organizations, they have carried on as before. Therefore, telling organizations that they need to approach their business from a different perspective is a bit like telling a smoker the dangers of smoking cigarettes. They know the dangers, they know that smoking will kill them, but they won't change their behavior.

Lots of psychologists will tell you all about conditioning, beliefs, values, and attitudes, which drive this seemingly complex arrangement of agreeing completely with the rationale, but refusing to change course. A bit like the Titanic captain who knew the ship was approaching the ice field and had been warned icebergs had been sighted, but still insisted on full steam ahead. The paradigm in which organizations are run is deeply engrained into the psyche of the people who lead them and the managers who manage them. Nothing changes, because deep down, the people running the businesses believe that if they keep doing what they will doing, they will achieve the revenue and income returns of yesteryear, not realizing that the business success and results of the past were based on meretriciousness.

Focusing on the Wrong Priorities

To be fair to the Senior Business Leaders, they probably have a hundred other priorities that they also know are really important but, given their limited resources they can only deal with five or six of the priorities with their current budgetary constraints. The biggest issue of course that, given the pressure to return dividends to shareholders, organizations are prioritizing dividend payments rather than investing profits back in the business (Rawlinson, 2015). It is the reason why many salaries have remained static, despite organizations profitability increasing. Shareholders are demanding more for less, and the big loser is investment in organizations resulting in lack of staffing and aging infrastructure. In the long term, this will result in catastrophic events, which will lead to lost revenue due to issues with customer service quality and failures. The recent IT failure, which caused BA to have a worldwide computer outage, stranding 75,000 passengers was probably caused by the company running outdated IT infrastructure that has reached the end of its life. The compensation is expected to cost the airline £100 million, the cost to its brand reputation has yet to be calculated.

So where does that leave us? It leaves organizations with a problem. Not only are they leaking investment out of the business, causing long-term sustainability issues, they are also focusing what little of the investment pots they have left on the wrong things. Part of my problem is that I passionately believe that it is People who are the key to organizational performance. If I didn't, I don't think I could do the job that I do. I fundamentally believe that people are an organizational asset that appreciates in value when invested in (correctly) and, more importantly, can deliver more to an organization than any capital asset, given the opportunity. With people, the sums really do result in $2 + 2 = 5$. Fundamentally, organizations only exist because of people. It is people who think up the product ideas, develop the design, and make the products. It is people who understand a need that can be met and design and deliver the service. It is people who come together to find a way to make something happen that may have been thought impossible once upon a time. We have air travel because people believed that it was possible to fly, and despite many failures, we can now board a plane that carries hundreds of people from one side of the world to the other. We can exchange information from one side of the world to the other in a blink of an eye because people worked out the hardware and software to make that possible. We can save lives because of medical advances, grow food in a desert, and cross oceans and ice sheets. We can have hot food in winter and cold drinks in summer all because of people. The computing power in our smart phones that we can hold in the palm of our hand is more powerful than the computers that sent a man to the moon at the end of the 1960s. When you think about the marvels of human endeavor, we truly are an extraordinary species.

If organizations were able to harness just one small speck of human ingenuity in their day-to-day operations, imagine what could be possible. And yet, all this potential and possibility is lost to organizations. Organizational leaders fret and worry about the EBITDA, capital utilization, and marginal cost and overlook the one asset that can, and does consistently create every day miracles.

What is more, the people asset doesn't stand still. Get the recruitment and talent management right in an organization, and someone recruited at entry level could one day end up running the company—think of that for a moment in regards to Return on Investment. You employ someone in a job worth a salary of $18 thousand a year, and 10 years later they are performing a job role worth $1 million a year. There are very few assets, which can accrue value in the same way, or indeed fundamentally change and add value in a different area and in a different way. Training investment isn't the same as uploading the latest software into the computer, or developing new processes, which, once they have been delivered remains static until the next upgrade or update. Learning expands, morphs, and mutates as the learner collects new learning, responds to experiences, gains additional knowledge, or is placed within a different context. It is never wasted or lost; rather it is symbiotic and exponential.

The Contribution that People Assets Make

The result of our learning is individuals working together who have ideas that contribute millions of dollars to an organization's bottom line because of new product or service ideas, process improvements, new business, or improvements. Every organization is a result of its people. Its successes are a sum of its parts, a result of people working together to deliver something truly amazing. Facilitating development workshops grants me privileged access of seeing the creativity process in motion, the moments when light bulbs light up, and innovation is sparked as one idea is built on with another and another until a truly magnificent moment is achieved and a creative outcome is delivered. These results aren't a once in a lifetime occurrence; they happen every time a group of people comes together with purposeful endeavor. The end result is millions of dollars of added value in improved productivity and the opening up of new markets, product, and services.

At this point, it would be remiss of me to avoid the negative aspect of my assertion. I acknowledge that the opposite is true, sometimes $2 + 2 = -5$ because someone screws up, and that's the rub for organizations. People are a risky asset. Just as they may add real value, so too can they destroy a company. Whether it is a mistake or a malicious intent, people are also the cause of all the organization's problems too. Yes, all of them. It is people who make the decisions that lose millions of dollars. It is people who ignore the processes, which result in health and safety violations. It is people that sell out, annoy customers, break things, and destroy good will. Just as they can add value, they can destroy it too. Also, one of the main reasons that I am brought into an organization to facilitate development workshops is because of dysfunctional teams. Senior leadership teams, who should really know better, failing to work together, refusing to let go of petty disagreements, colliding over which direction they believe the organization should travel in or in all out conflict, warring over politics, power, and personality clashes.

However, despite these things all being true, I honestly believe that most people, with very few exceptions, come to work to do a good job. They genuinely want to deliver something amazing. I am an advocate of McGregor's Theory Y assuming that individuals will show initiative, should be involved in decision making, ideally at the lowest level in the organization that it is safe to do so, that people are self-motivated, and that they will be creative and imaginative in their problem solving. People want to do well in work, but very often the organizational environment is not conducive to that being possible. Whether it is processes or policy that prevent people from doing the right thing, managers lacking the capability to help release individual potential or organizational structure that prevents cooperative and collaborative working, I have found that the root cause of problems caused by people is usually systemic rather than something that boils down to a single individual choosing to perform poorly. If an organization invested in its people, and invested resource in helping people do their jobs rather than in processes and policies that prevent people from being effective, then positive outcomes are assured.

Creating an Environment for Sustainable Performance

As an organization development practitioner, I meet many senior business leaders who have a genuine desire to create an environment for sustainable performance, but, at the same time, are reluctant to spend any money investing in their people asset. There is little chance, without investment and support, that people will be able to make a positive contribution. If they are not trusted to take pride in their work, and are micromanaged, then there is little scope for people to deliver any value to the organization. When it comes to investing in people resource, I find myself coming back to the advice on strengths. An organization should invest 80 percent of its resource in its strengths. An organization needs to invest in its infrastructure, but limiting the investment in its people, or not investing in people at all is a failure to follow the strengths investment principle. Taking a market view, the only asset that an organization has that cannot be replicated by its competitors is its people. It is the asset that gives the organization its competitive advantage. Every other asset innovation can be replicated, copied, or plagiarized. In a previous role, I worked for a soft drink manufacturer, who was a market leader, and as such invested heavily in research and development. Competitors would copy every flavor, product range, and even bottle design that the manufacturer developed within six months of its launch. The brand reputation was an important component, but on the supermarket shelf, the products were homogenous and the product line was commoditized. Keeping ahead of the competition was down to the constant innovation from both the product team and the marketing department. Fortunately, the organization did invest heavily in their people, and I would argue this is the reason it always kept one step ahead of the competition.

An organization knows that if it doesn't invest in its plant, then the likelihood of it running at optimum efficiency over the long term is low, and yet this is exactly what happens with the people asset. Also, as explored in the introduction, when training is given, so often the focus is on an individual's weak areas. Since a business would not invest all its marketing money on a product that was its weakest product, it seems illogical that it would pursue this course of action with its people resource. It seems that senior business leaders treat people in the exact opposite way of the most sensible and rational approaches that they use to build a business. It is by focusing on investing in the strengths of individuals and freeing up individuals to play those strengths at every opportunity that the organization will be able to deliver $2 + 2 = 5$.

The ROI from learning and development is not something that is impossible to measure. Many development practitioners will fret over the ROI of their development programs. Coming from a commercial background, I feel confident aligning what it is that the learning and development program needs to deliver with the outcomes that the organization is seeking. Investing in personal development is an opportunity to align individuals with an organization's purpose and develop mutually beneficial outcomes. Fundamentally seeking to answer the "So what?" for both the organization and the individual leads to the development of a solution, which will deliver something of worth to the organization. If the development program is worth more to the organization to run the program than not, then you have begun to build the business case for running a development program.

Investing in people is not a zero sum game that loses touch with the commercial business needs of the organization. At the same time as designing a great learning program, it is possible to start building in measures taking account the difference it will make to the organization if people develop in a particular area, what does that impact, and what will be different. Quite simply, if the learning and development deliver a change, which is visible, then you can see something, and if you can see something, you can measure it, if you can measure it, you can put a value against it. Therefore, not only can a business case can be built that demonstrates that $2 + 2 = 5$, and the organization committed to investing in people as the most important business asset should be developed, then it will deliver a measurable ROI, the value added will remain embedded in the business culture, and the organization will achieve more than it would do, if it continued to hope that that doing nothing will deliver fantastic results.

Manage Your Career Tool #3 – Personal Development Planning

Personal development planning (PDP) has got a fairly bad reputation, mainly because it is given scant regard during the performance development review session or because they get put in a drawer for a year and none of the development objectives succeed to leaving the PDP and making it into real life. Well as with all plans, the PDP is only as good as the investment put into, and the actions taken to implement it. Worthy of note is also to highlight that a PDP must be owned by the individual, as I once had to point out to a Finance Director, it's a *personal* development plan, which means that it is particular to the individual, who will get much more out of it if they take responsibility for it.

It is important that clear SMART objectives are set, and that the development goes beyond training courses and focuses on developing in all four key areas:

- Behaviors – How you act
- Experience – What you know
- Skills – What you can do
- Thinking Range – Your talent. Who you are.

Your task is to revisit the strengths statements that you wrote for Career Tool #2 and develop a PDP to increase the added value that can you achieve for the organization. Set yourself a maximum of three robust stretch development goals that you can focus on. This PDP should be an iterative exercise, which is constantly updated; as you finish one development action, you should set yourself another. Your goal should be continuous development and a growth mindset. A growth mindset is a belief that you can learn and become smarter and be better at what you do; it is a self-belief that you can be all that you are meant to be with hard work and perseverance. (Dweck, 2006)

Task 1 – Personal Development Planning

Development Objective	Actions	Responsibility	Time Frame	Measure of Success
For example – Have a Fierce Conversation With manager	Discuss feelings of frustration, disengagement (lack of enthusiasm) and 'take over' issues with manager in a 1-2-1 'over coffee' situation	CF	By the end of week commencing 01/10/2017	Clarity and reassurance over position

CHAPTER 3

A Name, Not a Number

Sometimes I lie awake at night and ask why me? Then a voice answers nothing personal, your name just happened to come up.

—Charles M. Schulz

Names. Everyone has one, most people have a vague idea what their own name means, but few of us give much thought to names and their importance in our life. Onomastics, the study of names, is a field that traverses a variety of disciplines including linguistics, history, anthropology, psychology, sociology, and philology. When people refer to the "meaning of a name", they are most likely referring to the etymology, which is the original literal meaning of the word. The historical significance of your name can be fascinating, but, in reality, the words that join together to give you a label that people call you tells you very little about who you are, your past, present, or your future. At most, it might tell you what your parents were thinking about; their hopes, fears, and dreams for you, at the time of your birth or the panic that overwhelmed them when writing your name on the birth certificate.

My name isn't actually my name, not legally anyway. To my friends, family, colleagues, and clients, I am Carrie. On the front of this book, the author's name is printed as Carrie Foster. It is what I am known as. However, to the passport office, DVLA, doctors, solicitors, mortgage company, and banks, I am Caroline; which can be confusing and disconcerting when I am faced with an official demanding my personal details and I struggle to correctly answer the first question they ask; "name" or stutter over what my own name actually is.

I was first called Carrie by my form tutor when I was 12 years old and despite being called Caz by my Mum, Dad, and brothers, I chose to be 'known as' Carrie, when I started work in my first 'proper' job after leaving university. As names go, there is nothing wrong with the name Caroline, which means free man, other than the haunting memory of it being screeched loudly by my Mum who used my full moniker to call me to attention when I was in trouble, which was often. My proper name, as opposed to my known name, therefore, somehow seems formal and comes with the added stress of only being used on forms and for legal transactions. Carrie has become more than my professional name, it is the name that I have chosen for myself, it is who I am.

Names are needed for several reasons. Firstly, they help us to distinguish ourselves from one another, which becomes more difficult if you have a team with three people who share a name, but is easier than asking to speak to the short brown-haired chap who deals with human resources. Names, therefore, separate who we are and identify us from those that we share space with and allow us to know when it is us that a personal interaction is being directed at. Nicknames are given as a form of endearment of insult. They have the power to add a description, positively or negatively, about someone as a person. This might be a reference to their appearance such as 'Little John,' their pecking order in a family or group setting; 'junior' or 'governor' or similarly their character 'Mad Tony.' Some names carry information about our roots, such as family or clan names, which are generally inherited, or reflect trends and fashions of the time. Carrie was a popular name in the 1970s because of Carrie Fisher's role in Star Wars. I am a child of the 70s, so, therefore, the moniker for me has connotations of a strong woman fighting for a just cause. And yes, I do sometimes get mail addressed Fisher instead of Foster. Other names have negative connotations and are best left to history. Children of parents who committed fiendish acts very often change their name or surname to disassociate themselves with their history. The name Adolf was fairly common before the Second World War, increased in popularity during the war, and then disappeared almost completely in the years since. Interesting fact, any associations with Nazism are pretty much frowned upon, so even car license plates avoid the letters SS and AH.

So names matter, and it isn't just your forename and surname, but the names you are known as. Online handles and usernames, names in email addresses, and anything that you use as an identifier has an impact on how you are perceived by people. Calling your twitter account @BigBoyChops has consequences as to how you perceived by other people perusing your online footprint. Sometimes, your name might not be available, but you do need to understand that the online world is a public space. Think about what impression your colleagues might have if you had your online handle instead of your real name on your identity badge at work. If it's an impression you would rather not give, then it is time to change. The same is true for email addresses. At school, it might be funny to have an email address that has your address as mentalspace@email.address.com, but this might not go down very well with potential recruiters, if it is typed out at the top of your curriculum vitae or resume.

Engaging with Who You Are

Sometimes, of course, you name isn't one that you would necessarily choose for yourself. Perhaps you are one of those people who has to live with an annoying name that becomes a butt of other people's jokes, such as Hugh Man, Al E. Gater, Joe King, or Kay Oss. As a parent, choosing a name that your child will be stuck with for the rest of their lives is a big responsibility. We called my son, Ioan, which is pronounced Yo-anne. The fact that I even have to explain how the name is pronounced should have been a warning that perhaps the choice of name for our eldest son was misdirected. We had good reason for choosing the name. We live in Wales and wanted a good Welsh name, and discovered the name through the Welsh actor, Ioan Gruffudd. It means chosen by God, and is the Welsh version of the name John, which happens to be my Father's first name, so seemed the perfect choice. My son is growing up fast, and part of me winces when other people say his name. Ewan or Johan are common mispronunciations, and I regularly witness the flicker of a wince and exasperation as he once again has to correct someone, or complains later that eventually he gave up with someone who just didn't get it right, all day. His friends call him Yo-Yo, which is a play on his name, but also suitably describes his inability to sit still, rather than being a reference to him having a temperament that is up and down. What I do know is that every time he introduces himself for the first time, people end up saying "Pardon?" After which he has to repeat his name several times before the new acquaintance gets it and he can move on from the greeting phase of a meeting. I now realize that I have burdened him with the experience of his name being misheard and mispronounced for the rest of his life. It doesn't help that he also has a double-barreled surname, that has also got a Welsh spelling and has to be carefully relayed over the phone to avoid the repeated mistake of too many or too few letters being included. As parents, we have lumbered him with forename and a surname, which no one can pronounce or spell. He will curse us every time he has to fill in an official form, or spell his name out, again and again, over the phone. However, this does have a positive side effect. It draws out the greeting process, so the people he is meeting for the first time have to pay attention and cannot get away with a cursory acknowledgement whereby they quickly forget who you are. They are forced to engage properly, and, in having to repeat his name, and get their mouth around the pronunciation the interaction means they take notice. They place the face with the name. His 'too long name' may be an annoyance at school when writing his name out on official forms or attempting to fit it onto a school jumper label, but it does call attention to him.

Finally, for my son, it has taught him to pay attention to others. When greeting people for the first time, he leans in, and listens closely to ensure he gets the name right. This courtesy is one we can all learn from. Our names are important, they serve an important social function, it only take a few extra seconds and a moment of concentration to hear someone's name properly. Knowing someone's name and using their name is important. In my role as facilitator or tutor, I am regularly confronted with situations where everyone in the room knows my name because they only have one name to learn, and I am still trying to figure out everyone's name at lunchtime. I am reasonably good at remembering names, but I hate being in the situation where I miss someone's name on introduction and it has passed the point of politeness to ask them to remind me. Worse still is where I muddle someone's name up. Recently, there was a participant called Andy and, in my head, his name was Ieuan. I worked with the group over a twelve-month period, and I still continued to get his name wrong. He accepted my inability to get his name right with good grace. I suppose the fact that I was calling him the same wrong name consistently perhaps helped him realize that I remembered who he was even if the name I'd labeled him with was wrong. As a development practitioner, I do, however, believe that remembering names is important.

It acknowledges that you have 'seen' that person in the widest sense of its meaning. In the Avatar movie, the phrase 'I see you' means I bring you into existence and for me that is what a name does in our society. In our society, our names bring us as a person into existence within the social setting, and, for that reason, we shouldn't treat someone's name disrespectfully or disdainfully.

Our Identity Is Tied to Our Name and Our History

A mistake is only a mistake if you don't learn from it. So when choosing my daughter's name, we steered away from Welsh names and chose Lily Grace. It's not double-barreled because, like my son she has been lumbered with a double-barreled surname, so we thought a double-barreled forename and surname was going a little bit overboard. However, Grace is not a middle name; it is the second part of her forename, although it often gets dropped. I now find myself calling her Lily Grace when disciplining her, and Lily at other times, along with a number of nom de plumes including sweetheart, sausage, and lulu. Which perhaps proves that we all turn into our parents in the end. But annoyingly, even members of my family still can't spell her name right, inscribing Lilly as a shortened version of Lillian on birthday and Christmas cards. There's only two L's for goodness sake, she's a Lily like the flower, meaning pure. The mis-pronounciation or mis-spelling of names teaches us something important about how our identity is tied up in our name. I have heard people say "she/he looks like a [insert name]" and I often wondered what assumptions are made about a person to make such a statement possible. But, regardless as to whether Lily Grace and Ioan look like their names, their name now has a meaning beyond what is written in the history of names book. Who we are as people is associated with the name by which we go by. Caroline is, in my mind, associated with being naughty and getting into trouble. Carrie is by the same token a professional businesswoman. They are separated in my mind as much as I am separated by time from my childhood self. I am no longer that person even though my birth certificate very plainly identifies me as such. My parents still believe that I am like my childhood self, even though I have changed and grown to be the adult that I am today.

Circumstances have knocked the rough edges from me, and learning about myself, and engaging in self-development practices have taught me to temper some of my negative traits and foster my strengths. The danger for us as individuals is crossing paths with people from our past who engage with us as if we were still the person they knew way back when. Shakespeare wrote a speech which is referred to as the seven ages of man, which captures the changing position of an individual through the different stages of their life: infant, schoolboy, early youth, the obligations of late youth, the justice sought in adulthood, the slowing down into middle age, and the frailty of old age as we face our death. As we traverse life, it becomes apparent that we do change who we are as we get older, and possibly wiser. The cares and worries of our youth are replaced with changing ideas as we learn more about life, and ourselves. We carry part of who we are at each stage of life, into the next, but we do change and some people change more than others. Unfortunately, people from our past make assumptions about our character, and who we are based on their knowledge of us. However, we are different. Imagine someone who used a computer during the 1970s, and then did not use a computer again until today. The machine is still a computer, but its functionality is leaps ahead; for a start, we don't need floppy discs to start the computer and the hard disk capacity has increased millions of times over. In many ways, the new generation of computing is a completely new thing. As human beings, our development is of a similar trajectory. As we learn, grow, and experience new things, we change and evolve. Some experiences are what Mezirow (1990) termed as transformative learning, they fundamentally change our understanding of ourselves, our beliefs, and convictions about what is true and the way we live our lives. Therefore, although our name may remain the same, our identity is flexible. Unlike a number, which remains fixed in meaning, our identity can change, and with it the experience people have of you.

Capturing What You Are About

When I started my first business, a training consultancy, I had to choose a name for the business. Most of the advice I read about naming a business said that you should call your consultancy after your own name, something along the lines of 'Foster Consultancy,' but I didn't find that particularly inspiring. I found choosing a name for my business was difficult. I needed to get it right because potential clients would infer a lot from the name and first impressions count, and being a limited company meant I couldn't just choose any name because it might be registered by someone else and, in the digital age, I had to also consider availability of website names too. At the time I wanted a name that captured what my business was about, building capability to perform, and so Fortitude Development was born. It was a good solid name, but the name doesn't make it obvious what services I offered, giving me scope to change and flex according to what opportunities came my way. More than that though the business name was a statement of purpose. It drew a line in the sand regarding the type of business I wanted to have and the reason why the business existed in the first place. I also had to choose a title for myself. As a Director, I could choose to call myself anything I wanted; but let's be honest, the consultancy hasn't exactly got 1,000 employees, so my job title doesn't really represent my 'day job'. Some years later and the season of Fortitude Development came to an end. My work has moved away from fortitude to a greater focus on Organization Development and writing. My job title has also changed. I now label my job role as 'Woman of Many Businesses,' a reflection perhaps, not only of the fact that my pathway is constantly changing, but a confidence in who and what I am.

What I do know is that when I was younger, my job title mattered a great deal, and as a young graduate in my first corporate role I was striving for the job title of manager; as I have got older, I have realized that the only name that really matters is my name, Carrie. What my business is called, what my job title is, is actually irrelevant. My business is who I am, it is my identity that enables me to sit at my laptop and share my thoughts and ideas with you, or stand in front of a leadership team and support them in their learning journey and team development or perhaps working on a large whole organization intervention coopting employees to deliver value for their organization. One of my clients suggested that my business was carrie.com, since what I am doing is an extension of my identity, of who I am, just as my name is an extension of the legal person that my birth certificate certifies. For me, this is the epitome of the challenge to be and not to do. My authenticity of self is because I am fully myself in the work that I turn my hand to. In my youth, I would put on a suit, and with it play a character. Today, I am what I am, the good bits and the bad bits. The difference is, that my identity is not threatened by the work that I do, instead I am comfortable in the skin I am in. Criticism and feedback are received in the spirit with which it is given and doesn't threaten my understanding of who I am. I am more relaxed and more at peace, I still have the same drive and enthusiasm about the work I do, but there is a calmness because I am not trying to prove that I am something that I am not. The closer you can get to authenticity in the workplace, the happy you will be. It is a choice you can make. To be who you really are, or to settle for a social construction of who other people think you should be.

The same is true when taking on roles and responsibilities. We don't have to pretend that we can do something that we can't. When I first started my business, my mobile phone provider suggested I speak to our IT department when I was struggling to get my work email connected to my smartphone. I told the customer service representative of the phone company that my IT department were pretty useless, and they should all be sacked. I have since outsourced IT to friends and my husband when I can't work things out for myself. Very often at work, we feel that we can't say we can't, that we somehow have to be good at everything and deliver outside of our abilities. The Peter Principle (Peter, 1969) states that individuals are selected during interview or for promotion based upon their ability to do their current role. Therefore, individuals eventually reach their level of incompetence when they are promoted to a role beyond their capabilities. When I work with dysfunctional organizations, I very often find individuals in management who were brilliant in their previous roles, but have been promoted into a role that they aren't able to do, and that they end up doing a very bad job in. These managers not only feel stuck and frustrated, but do an awful lot of damage to the people who are reporting to them. It is, therefore, incumbent upon us, as individuals, to be honest about our capabilities. Now, of course, you might not know you can't do something until you try, realistically that is what secondment and project roles are for. The onus, however, is to admit when we can't do something, or when something sits outside our area of talent. At the same time, organizations need to not condemn people for being honest about the limit of their capabilities, and also provide opportunities for individuals to grow in their current position. Hierarchical organizational structures have prevented this honesty, but the measure of success in regards to your career development isn't whether you have got the fancy title or the big pay packet. Instead success is about whether you are being fully you within your own position.

The Evolving Nature of a Job Makes Job Titles Redundant

The name jobs are given is absurd anyway. A few years ago, I studied my MA in Human Resource Management. During my studies, we explored the transition from Personnel, to Human Resources to Strategic Human Resources. Research shows that as the name has changed, it has been followed by changes in the professionalism and focus of the HR function and people working in the department. I have noticed in my own field of practice that there was a transition about 10 years ago from Training and Development to Learning and Development, and, more recently, many development professionals have been given the moniker of Organization Development. Along with it has been a change in responsibility, an alignment with the business strategy, and a widening of focus to a more holistic and humanistic approach to development, but many Organization Development Directors are still operating as training and development officers. These transitions aren't limited to the people side of the organization either. When I started my career, I was a sales representative. Today, you have customer relationship managers, account managers, and business development consultants because the job role has shifted from selling to partnering with clients. Factory managers are now operations managers as silos are broken down and the interconnected nature of the job role has been understood and utilized. Sometimes, the job title change will come first, alongside a shift in job role responsibilities; but even when this structural change happens, you notice that most individuals grow into their job title and then, over time, begin to outgrow their job title. My view, therefore, is that we should look beyond titles and instead focus on what it is the individual is doing. Very often, a job role morphs and changes over a period of time, to such an extent that the job description and job name bear very little resemblance to the work being done. Like our own name, therefore, assumptions cannot be made about the character of the work that a person does; however, as explored in the introduction, of all the components of our professional life, our job label matters. The organization's name, the individual's name, and our job titles have a significant influence. Almost from the moment it is first written down, a name begins impacting perceptions, traits, and talents. With time, the vibration of the name plays a major role in establishing relationship patterns and communication style.

Names, therefore, aren't just labels or mere words of identification; they take on a whole new energetic purpose and reality. They create a personality for the organization, for the individual, and for the role holder. A name is a thing of great power that molds who we are and who we will become. So choose wisely.

Manage Your Career Tool #4 – Developing Your Identity

Developing an understanding or self-awareness of who we are begins with a process of self-inquiry. Your understanding of your identity, the words you would choose to describe yourself drive our perception of self, and our subsequent behavior based on that perception. Self-awareness requires you to reflect regularly on yourself and your actions to understand why you do what you do. This can be achieved by asking powerful questions to grow your understanding of self and deepen your awareness.

Developing your identity is not a one-time thing. It is an iterative process, of constant inquiry, which needs to be repeated at regular intervals. Moon (2004) states that "reflection is a type of thinking aimed at achieving better understanding and leading to new learning." Because we change, our self-perception will change over time. Being aware of what those changes mean, and whether those changes require us to take a different direction are an important part of developing our learning process and will help us to develop self-confidence and authenticity in the workplace. Most important of all is that we must be honest about what we are thinking and feeling and we need to find an outlet in which we can express ourselves. Strong emotions are toxic if they are bottled up, and can lead to negative consequences such as tension and stress, both at the workplace and at home.

Regularly writing down your thoughts in a personal learning journal provides you with an opportunity to explore, reflect, and make decisions based upon what you truly think and feel.

- Who am I in this situation and is it who I want to be?
- Why do I feel this way?
- What is the origin of some of the thoughts and feelings that I have?
- What assumptions am I making about a situation/person, and are these assumptions true?
- What further information do I need to avoid false assumptions?
- Who could I speak to get clarification?
- Why am I doing what I am doing?
- What is the main purpose behind my actions?
- Am I losing sight of the bigger picture?
- What would happen if I stopped what I was doing and did something else instead?
- What is the most important thing for me right now, this week and this month?

It is recommended that you make self-inquiry a habit. This means setting time aside, preferably at the same time each week to exercise self-inquiry and reflection. If you like stationary, take time to select a beautiful journal, but taking the time to reflect and capture your thoughts and ideas is what is really important.

CHAPTER 4

Why You Matter

Whatever you do may seem insignificant to you, but it is most important that you do it.

—Mahatma Gandhi

It does matter what you do with the life you have been given. You might have experienced a terrible upbringing, told by teachers that you would never amount to anything, or you might have had the opposite experience, encouraged to achieve great things and loaded down with expectations about what you should be doing. We cannot change what has happened in the past. We cannot change our upbringing or wave a magic wand to take away experiences that have hurt us or damaged us in anyway. There is no going back. But what happens from here on is, in your decision, your choice, and in your power to make different. It doesn't matter if you are a complete screw up, and you have made bad decisions and huge mistakes. Whether you have self-destructed or pushed the implode button. What is done, cannot be undone. There is, however, time to do something different, to make different choices. Regardless of your age, your life choices, or your career history, you can start afresh. There is time to step out and step up, for no other reason than because you can, and because who you are matters.

For many people trying to work out what it is that we are here to do is a major question. If you are stuck in a job you don't like, working long hours and working extremely hard trying to prove your value to an organization that doesn't appreciate the talent you have, the experience can be demoralizing and demotivating. Worse still is if the manager or organization doesn't treat people as anything more than a resource to be deployed and measured. It can feel like you have no worth, no talent, and nothing that you do or say really matters. Every person who ends up believing this lie is a loss to the world. Imagine if Martin Luther King, Albert Einstein, Thomas Edison, or Charles Babbage believed that they had nothing to offer. Sometimes, we can look at the greats and think that our lives don't matter as much as theirs did, but every person has a unique and special contribution to make to the world we live in. Even if you are not the next Einstein, it may be that the part you have to play in life creates the opportunity or touch point that galvanizes the next Einstein to achieve something amazing. You might never know how much the role you play mattered in the creation of something that is awesome. A word at the right time, a smile when someone felt that no one cared, the provision of coffee that fuels the innovator, the drive in the cab to that all-important meeting, the accident that led to a happenstance. You don't know what impact your life interacting with others will lead to and that is why you matter. It isn't just about what you do, but who you are in every little moment that creates magic.

A Waste of Talent

Too often we play our lives as if we don't matter and in situations where you are treated like you don't, it is hard work trying to find your value where you aren't valued. We might not all be presidents or leaders. We might not command the world stage or invent a world-changing product or service, but we were all put on earth for a reason. Regardless of your religious beliefs, your birth was not an accident. You are the result of billions of interactions and events that led to your conception. That isn't luck or chance. You are here, right now, because this is the right time for you to be here. We live in a world where people are made to feel like they don't matter and that their lives are worthless than someone else's by fate of fortune and circumstance. The levels of depression are higher now than at any other time, even during the war years. Individuals feel that they are stuck in jobs because there appears to be no other option. The War for Talent is only being fought for the top two per cent of employees in an organization, which leaves 98 percent of people with talents that are ignored by the organization where we spend a large proportion of our lives. What a waste. Personally, I think that performance management and talent management in organizations spend most of its time on wasting the talent that is available to the organization. Strategic Talent Management has such a limited focus on future leaders' programs that it forgets that the rest of their employee population has a huge amount of talent that isn't even close to being tapped into, and even worse, is being destroyed as people lose the opportunity and confidence to be everything that they are made to be. Imagine if you owned a property where you only invested in one room. Of all the rooms in the entire house there is only this one room that ever gets decorated or maintained. What happens to the rest of the rooms in the house? To begin with, not a lot, they might get a bit dusty, and fusty, but they are still usable and serve their purpose. Now, fast forward five years, what does the room look like now, or how about in ten years? Unrecognized talent in people is like the unused rooms in the house. Without investment or use, the talent sits collecting dust, and if skills and knowledge aren't invested in, they begin to decay.

Organizations should invest in all their people, and although some people who are key strategic talent may get a greater level of investment, it would be criminal to leave any talent unused or underutilized. Some organizations are waking up to that fact and realizing that they need to prioritize people development, but for many organizations, developing their employees isn't even on the agenda, let alone a priority. If an organization were to manage its other resources the same way it manages its people, it wouldn't be in business very long, and the shareholders would be appalled at the small percentage of return on assets. The problem is that people aren't like capital equipment. For a start, we aren't standardized and we also evolve over time, so the person an organization recruits will not be the same as the person who is still working for the organization three years later. There are also a lot of variables outside the control of the organization; the external environmental factors that impact an individual's performance are very difficult to scan for. A rogue boyfriend, a pregnant wife, a cheating partner, the loss of a loved one—don't need to be factored into the risk analysis for a piece of equipment.

You Need to Own Your Talent Development

The emphasis for liberating talent, therefore, falls on the individual. For the majority of employees, the only way in which their true potential can be released is either if they realize for themselves how great they are or they are fortunate enough to be managed by a rare breed, a line manager who is interested in developing their people. The first stage of course is to take ownership of your talent development. Firstly, you have talent, even if you don't know the full extent of it yet. Secondly, it is within your power to develop it. The rise of Massive Open Online Courses (MOOCs) and the growth of forums, how-to videos, and free training activities means that you do not need a student loan big enough to buy a house to develop your knowledge or skills set. What you do need is a determination that you will develop yourself, and a willingness to put time resource aside to achieve it. If you are working two jobs and have a family to look after, this is hard. I'm not going to pretend that adding one more thing to your million and one things to do isn't burdensome. If you do choose to go to college and study for a qualification or attend a night school course, it eats into your personal down time and your personal finances. Therefore, investing in your talent is a decision you have to make, realizing that there is a cost associated with that decision. It might mean several years of struggling by, making sacrifices to get where you want to get to. However, if you choose not to make that commitment, then you are choosing to stand still. Not making a decision is still a choice. Waiting for someone else to develop you might result in the slim chance that an organization will be willing to invest in you. In my experience though, it is usually those people who invest in themselves that attack investment from organizations.

There are many reasons why you wouldn't take part in self-development activities, and most of them are valid reasons. Very often when developing individuals, I find that they feel paralyzed by their circumstances, feeling stuck, and with no options. We aren't taught how to identify, develop, and manage our talent potential and managers are rarely taught how to identify, develop, and manage the talent potential of the people they are managing. One of the first things an individual needs to develop is an understanding of what and how to develop the areas they need to develop. My personal view on this is that it requires communication with other people. Mentoring has often got a bad reputation, mainly because executive coaches like to point out the difference between mentoring and coaching with the emphasis on how great coaching is as an intervention, and coaching is a great intervention, if you have access to a coach. But first things first, a mentor can be anyone. Ideally, it will be someone who has some sway and influence in helping you achieve your dreams. This might be a senior leader in your organization or someone with a good reputation in your industry. Equally, it might be a former teacher that you found helpful at high school, a valued ex-employer who helped you get your foot on a ladder, a friend of the family, or a respected person in your community. There is no one size or shape of a mentor that makes them right or wrong. What does make them right for you is that they are someone you get on with personally, that they will give you wise council, they have experience that you can learn from (even if it's not directly related to your field) and, in an ideal world, they have connections which can open doors for you. Finally, they must be willing to give time for mentoring you, meeting for coffee and conversation on a regular basis. By coopting a mentor at the beginning of your development journey, you will be able ask questions, get support, and receive guidance, which helps with the next steps.

Finding Talent Directions

In Career Tool#2, we explored how to identify strengths, but strengths are only part of the equation. You can be very good at something, even enjoy doing it, but you wouldn't want to make it a full-time job. For example, I am very good at lecturing, and, when I am lecturing I enjoy the interaction with students. However, although I occasionally work at the local university, it's not what I want to do as a career. There is a lot of peripheral things around the teaching profession that I don't enjoy at all, and I don't feel a calling to be a full-time lecturer. Although not always the case, talent directions are usually linked to those things that we are passionate about; but very often passion is left for our spare time or dreams and rarely considered as being a career option. When I work as a career coach with people, I am often struck by how our dreams are sucked out of us from an early age, and we consign our dreams to get a proper job. It seems strange to me that we give up on doing what we dream of doing because it isn't a real option and yet, there are people in world who are doing what you want to do.

From the age of seven, I wanted nothing more than to write. I'd spend hours writing in exercise books, making up stories and even, during my teenage years, writing poetry. Whether it was that I had watched too much Wonder Woman on television, I had a dream to be a journalist and drive a burgundy open top car. I don't know why the car was important, but it was part of my vision for my career. Throughout my education, I pursued this dream. I sought out opportunities to get involved with journalism, doing work experience at the local newspaper, and even interviewing the then British Prime Minister, John Major, when he came to visit my school. I was focused and determined on my goal. Then, during the summer between school and university, I worked at the Sunday Times, a well-respected newspaper in the UK. After I finished my work experience, I realized that, if this was the pinnacle of my chosen career, it wasn't for me. I went off to university without a plan, having laid down writing as a career choice and no longer clear on what future I was working toward. I fell into a sales career after university and then made a career change into people development. It was only when I began my own business that I started writing again. Nearly twenty years had passed without me doing any writing beyond that required for writing reports and presentations. It began with blogging, then a conversation with a colleague at the university led to a journal article, which was published, and then another, and another, and here were are, I am a published author, this is my day job, and I am living the driving. Okay, so the burgundy open top car is a Toyota Auris and its Tokyo Red. My path may have diverged from the one I had planned, but everything that I have done in the intervening years makes the writer I am today.

It could be argued that I got lucky, but those twenty years were filled with ups and downs, risks taken, failure and, at times, despair about whether I would ever do anything my life. I speak as someone who decided at the age of 30, well into a successful career, that if I was going to live my life, then I was going to be Carrie Foster instead of do a job. It didn't happen overnight, and there were times where my nose was so close to the hitting a brick wall, I wondered if I had destroyed everything. The question I ponder is whether it was worth it? as I sit here at my writing table, with an eye on a deadline, looking out at my garden, I am content that it was.

We Only Have One Life, and Yours Matters

Our lives are such a short period of time in the scheme of things, and our working lives take up a huge amount of the time we have on earth. If you are going to live this life, I mean really LIVE this life, why would you not want to spend your life doing something that makes you feel fulfilled? Why would you not choose to spend your life being everything you could be? Settling for the second best not only robs us of our opportunity to rise to our greatest level of potential, it robs the world of our brilliance played out in full. This isn't something that is the preserve of the rich and lucky. My life as an author has not been handed to me on a plate. It was hard work, and I lost many battles along the way. Some people, they do get lucky, and they do achieve things with seemingly little effort and, yes those who come from a wealthy background have the luxury of making choices that the rest of us do not have. So, if you are from a disadvantaged background, the valleys are deeper and mountains are harder to climb. There will be times when you will wonder whether the effort required to demand that your life is worth something is too high a price to pay. I can only speak from experience in telling you that it is worth fighting for.

Another thing to consider is the wider society in which we live in. Our wrong job might be the right job for someone else. By remaining in it, not only are we miserable, we are also potentially stopping someone else from stepping into their perfect role. My best friend loves working with animals, especially reptiles; that type of work would be my idea of hell. It might seem strange to you, but there are people out there who love what you hate doing. There are people born to be administrators, who love nothing better than creating order. Just because I get no pleasure from it, doesn't mean no one does. Equally, people will look at my chosen profession and can't think of anything worse.

You have been given a precious gift. The potential you have is too amazing to keep hidden, and your life too important to spend it doing something you hate. It is time to step out and take ownership of your talent potential, own your destiny, and live life.

What are you going to do with the life you have been given?

What can you do, but live?

You have been given breath and strength

And every day live.

—Paraphrased from Matt Redman (2006)

Manage Your Career Tool #5 – Purposeful Endeavor

A good question to ask yourself if you feel stuck in knowing what your purpose is, is: "What would you do if money, geography, knowledge, and skills were no barrier?"

_____

_____

_____

_____

_____

_____

_____

_____

_____

_____

Usually, the answer to this question produces a destination that is close to what you really want to do. By removing the stuff that gets in the way, it becomes easier to shape the passion that lies in your heart, to unearth what really matters. You might not have a job role in mind, just a random collection of things "I want to work with helping people to . . ." but reflecting on these ideas will help you begin to shape what it is you were put here to do. I encourage you to keep revisiting these ideas and working on them until the random thoughts become a concrete idea. Once you have a clearer idea of what your purpose is, you can begin working on a plan to make it a reality.

CHAPTER 5

Being Rather than Doing

From the time we're born until we die, we're kept busy with artificial stuff that isn't important.

—Tom Ford

A few years ago, I had the pleasure of visiting a school friend in Belgium for her birthday. On the Saturday night, we went to a thirty-plus party to celebrate. Basically, a thirty-plus party is like the parties we went to when we were at school; beer in plastic glasses, a DJ with one of those rigs with 'disco lights' on it, and music from the late 1980s and 1990s. Having hung up our coats on the coat rack (there was no cloakroom attendant), we spent the next three hours dancing as if we were eighteen years old again, finally leaving around two-thirty in the morning. It was only later that morning that a stiff back and sore knees ruefully (and rudely) reminded me that I am no longer eighteen. But, there was another significant difference other than the wrinkles that I noticed on our night out and that was related to our self-confidence. True, many of the thirty-plus year olds who were there were out on the pull that night, and many women and men were desperately trying to appear attractive. But we were there for laughs. We danced without caring what other people thought and ended up with our own little group of partygoers wanting to join our gang. We weren't interested, but for me it was interesting that other people were attracted to us because we were just being ourselves. Those living in Hasselt were possibly amused by the slightly kooky lady from Britain, who dressed to please herself rather than please others, given that most people there seem to dress in brown, grey, black, or navy blue. Bright raspberry denim and floral tops have only really started making an appearance this season in

Belgium, or so I am told, and I am not sure they were quite ready for my gold brogues, which are my dancing shoes of course.

I have found great success by being myself. I am extremely successful at being Carrie Foster, in fact, I'm fairly certain that I am the best person in the world at being me. It's funny how when growing up we pursue success in the same way we pursue love. We strive, and work, and do, and worry about trying to get something that is just out of reach and to be someone who is accepted and acceptable. As you get older, and maybe a little wiser, you begin to realize that being rather than doing what other people are doing is firstly more enjoyable, but also leads to greater success.

Be Rather than Should

I spend a lot of time creating leadership and management development programs, which help individuals to scrub away the things that they believe they 'should' do, which then become the things that they think they must do. My job, therefore, is to help leaders find who they are in order to find their own success. The result is greater success for the organization as individual performance improves and untapped potential is released.

It's not that we can't learn from other people, and by trying out what other people do we can find out more about who we are; but the danger occurs when we try to reach a form of societal expectation or be so like the other person that we stop being who we are. We can take inspiration from those around us, but we should only take ideas from what others do and make them our own. Borrow and blend rather than copy and pretend. Organizations are the same. Organizations, which try to copy what other organizations do in order to achieve success often, fail to achieve the success the other organization achieved, or fail completely by pursuing an agenda that is not compatible. It is good for organizations to benchmark themselves against leading organizations, and it is good to seek out best practice. But, it is dangerous to think that best practice is necessarily best practice for your organization. What you should be looking for is best fit.

There is a depressing statistic that I read somewhere that sixty percent of people are in jobs they hate. Sixty percent! The statistic is mindboggling. That means six in ten of us are working in a job role we not only would prefer not to be doing, but we actually hate. There is intensity to feeling hatred that goes beyond simply not wanting to do something. I mean, I don't like having to do some of the administration that comes with being self-employed, but I don't hate doing it. This then leads me to wonder why people have found themselves in a situation where their work is not just dissatisfying, but also it is positively despicable. Maybe, they have followed a career that their parents had mapped out for them, or they copied what their school friends were doing or, like most of us, fell into a career by accident and happenstance. It could be that having followed what other people were doing, that once they were on that career path, they never once stopped to ask whether it was the right career for them to follow.

Waste of Past Effort, or Waste Future Potential

Having been someone who changed career after realizing that the job I was doing didn't satisfy me, I can testify that it is not a particularly nice place to be. You invest a lot of time at work, and if you want to progress, you have probably invested time in training and developing your skills and knowledge in that area. To change careers now would seem like everything that has gone before was a waste of time and effort. The challenge is whether you continue doing something you hate, or you choose to bite the bullet and be something you are meant to be. Making the choice to be may mean taking a step down on your career trajectory. Certainly, when I chose to pursue people development as a career, I had to step down from being a sales manager and become a learning and development advisor. I had to take a step backwards to move forward. However, I progressed quickly, because of the transferable skills that I had developed in my sales career, including my management skills that meant that I was soon able to progress up the career ladder in my new profession, far quicker than I would have done if I'd started out in the profession without my previous experience. I also discovered that the commercial knowledge that I gained from being in sales stood me in good stead in the human resource profession; in fact, it became my unique selling point. I was more credible in my learning and development because of the previous career path. The things that I learnt in sales also added to my portfolio of skills, making me better at my job. Return on investment wasn't some intangible thing that many development professionals avoid, the concept is a core part of the way I approach designing my interventions. Networking, negotiation, writing the business case, evaluating the financial return; these skills and the knowledge I have were built in my sales career. Therefore, what I did in my previous career has shaped my practice in my new career. None of it was wasted. I am a success because of what I have done as a whole, not despite it.

I believe the worst thing that can happen is that you stop grasping the opportunity to be who you are, because you are afraid of letting go of something you are doing that is comfortable and safe, even if you hate it. I have learnt over the years that by being more myself, I can be the success I am looking for and be the change that I need in my life. The more I try to fit into a box, the more I am frustrated, and the more I am likely to fail. There are times when we have to conform and compromise in life. My marriage wouldn't have lasted seventeen years if I'd failed to compromise along the way. But, when there is more compromise than staying true to who you are, then the balance is wrong. You know when you are being true to yourself. There is smoothness and comfort to the way things work. You lose that feeling that you are pushing a rock up hill, and instead feel like you are free wheeling down a gentle slope. Even when things are difficult, or you have a deadline to hit, or things that aren't quite going right, if you are authentic to you and being instead of doing, even the hard bits are easy to bear.

Some of the most successful organizations create an environment where employees are encouraged to explore their potential to its fullest, where they are allowed to find out who they are and how who they are can contribute to the success of the organization. Without people, there is no organization. Allowing individuals to be who they really are will enable the individuals to be successful and help the organization to be successful too. Trying to fit square pegs in round holes leads only to friction and conflict. Finding ourselves in every walk of life not only allows us to dance freely, but also causes others to want to join in.

Manage Your Career Tool #6 – Dancing in Gold Shoes

Finding purpose at work might feel like the type of thing you need to be in a religious order to achieve. But, the word purpose has its origins in an Anglo-French word relating to an intent or putting something in place, and in design. In short, finding purpose is about designing something that fits perfectly to, like a good pair of shoes. Not everyone wants to dance in gold shoes, but finding a position where you work, which is an expression of who are, is the intent. Some questions to help you reflect on this are:

1. Ask yourself: "Who am I?" If you are an organization, ask: "Who are we?"
2. Then ask yourself: "Why am I here?" If you are an organization, ask: "What is our Purpose?"
3. Define your own measures of success, how will you know when you've got there?
4. Consider what is different about you that will give added value to other people, the job role, the organization, and even society as a whole.
5. Don't be afraid of being different, but rather celebrate it—it's your Unique Selling Point and will help bring you success.
6. Try things on for size, but if they don't fit, don't keep them.
7. Never feel you have to do something because someone else does, make sure you are doing something because it helps you reach achieve your purpose (see 2).
8. Encourage others who are pursuing purpose, and pass the encouragement on if you have benefited from being encouraged.
9. Don't be afraid of failure. John Wooden said "If you are not making mistakes, then you are not doing anything." At least you are endeavoring to be purposeful.
10. If you are a square peg, keep away from round holes. Trust your instinct, it's usually right.

These are big questions, which deserve our consideration and thoughtfulness. Don't feel afraid of not having all the answers, but pursue a process of seeking to finding them.

CHAPTER 6

Being Rather than Doing Will Make You Happy

Life is far too important a thing ever to talk seriously about.

—Oscar Wilde

When was the last time you caught yourself doing something that you love? Not just something you enjoy, or find amusing, or that is better than doing the paperwork, unless you really love paperwork, but something that completely fills you up from the inside, and lights you up like a Christmas. It goes beyond simply that it was nice; it involves regret when you walk away and a deep sense of contentment that you had been involved in that process. When you do something you love, it gives you a sense of fulfillment and feeling of self, which cannot be achieved merely by doing anything. Loving what you do stops what you are doing from being a task and instead causes you to be who you are, lost in the moment, and knowing that this, this thing is right, right now. No amount of money, job title, reward, or recognition can match that feeling. In fact, if it was not for the fact that you need to pay your bills, it would be something that you would willingly do for free.

It's Not About The Money

When it comes to being happy, salary has to be taken out the equation. Judge et al (2010) found that the link between salary and job satisfaction is very weak, being engaged with the work that you do isn't going to happen because you are paid well. In fact, the research by Deci et al (1999) found that incentives can have a negative effect on our enjoyment of a job. You should be remunerated for the work you do in a job because you are bringing all your skills, knowledge, and talent into the endeavor, but money cannot be given as a reason for the motivation behind why you to do what you do it. Now, many people reading this will not have the luxury to turn down paid work because it isn't motivating. Most of us work because we have bills to pay and need to keep a roof over our heads and food in our bellies. However, the decision to stay in a job you hate because of the pay will never make you satisfied. We are conditioned to believe that we need all the trappings of success to be happy. From the moment we are old enough to take in information, we are marketed to, persuaded, and influenced in order to convince us that if we just had the latest, greatest, most marvelous thing, then life would be truly wonderful. But what are we actually trying to achieve? There is the story about the businessman trying to persuade the fisherman on the beach to commercialize his fishing business and when asked why, it boiled down to becoming successful enough to enjoying sitting on the beach, something the fisherman was already achieving.

Too often we spend so long looking at what we don't have, we miss what we have already got. Therefore, money is a minor consideration versus working in a position where you are truly able to be yourself. It might mean making some hard choices about where you live, and the type of lifestyle that you enjoy, and you might think that you have worked hard to achieve these things that society tells us are so important. But, they are just things, and you can't take them with you, and is the enjoyment you get from these things really worth you working yourself into an early grave doing a job you hate and missing out on all the things you would love to do? It's a fundamental question about what yardstick we seek to measure success by.

What Is Success?

Some time ago, when I was experiencing one of those nose to the brick wall moments in my business, my family had a meal to celebrate my brother's birthday. We were struggling financially at the time, so much so, that my family ended up agreeing to fund our families travel costs and the cost of meal, so we could join the family celebration. During the meal, my Mother decided to toast her children. She started off with my eldest brother, who although had passed away, was a great success in his career and had achieved the position of Sales Director. Cheers. Then she talked about my middle brother who, at the time was a successful electronic engineer and a Project Director. Cheers. She then celebrated the recent promotion of my younger brother who had secured a position as a Director at a Bank. Cheers . . . and then there is Carrie . . . . Cheers. I do come from a family of high achievers, and I had given up a successful corporate career to be, rather than do a job. The situation I was in at the time was painful; by my family's standards, I was a failure, there were possibly even concerns that I had lost the plot and gone a little bit mad. Perhaps there is some truth in that and about twelve months later my first business failed, and that was a hard time to work through. But what is success? It's a question you need to ask yourself. What measuring stick are you using to determine whether you are successful or not? Whose measure of success are you trying to measure up to?

I have discovered success on my own terms; it doesn't come with a proper job title. I say I'm a Woman of Many Businesses because I can't quite decide what I want to be when I grow up. It also doesn't come with the usual trappings of success, and I rarely wear a suit. Confucius said "choose a job you love, and you will never have to work a day in your life." I truly love the work I do, and it rarely feels like a job. I occasionally pinch myself because I can't quite believe that people pay me for doing something that is far too enjoyable to call work. Yet growing up, I was led to believe that few people got to live the dream, that this was the preserve of the lucky few, and yet, more and more people I bump into have decided to redefine what success is and choose to be who they really are instead of do a job. Living in the fullness of your potential means it is not just job satisfaction that you experience, it is life satisfaction. I appreciate that pursuing a dream is risky, and many people pursue their dreams and fail. I address failure further in Chapter 12, so, for now, I will simply say that failure is an important part of our learning process, and shouldn't be feared, and also that you should never give up. In pursuing who you are, your definition of success will fall out of sync with societal norms of consumerism. It doesn't mean that you can't earn a decent salary, I now earn more than I did in corporate life, and it doesn't mean you can enjoy the fruits of your labor. But, it does mean that you don't need those things to feel successful.

For me, my measures of success are to do with seeing that moment when the light bulb goes off and I know that the person I am working with is changed forever, that they finally understand how amazing and brilliant they are, for the first time in their lives. It is the feeling I get when I submit a manuscript, finished to my satisfaction for editing, and it is seeing the transformation in an organization and chatting with the senior management team as a trusted advisor because they have experienced how the stuff that I do using organization development delivers the change they were hoping for. Those are moments that motivate me to get out of bed at 4:15am on a Monday morning to get the train to London to deliver a day of coaching. It's what keeps me going when I experience a bout of writer's block and worry about missing a deadline, and it is what makes me push through when Chief Executives are suspicious as to whether 'playing with Lego' will deliver a return on investment. I can articulate these measures of success because I have worked out what really makes me tick, and what really makes me happy.

Doing What You Love in Corporate Life

In organizational life, the point in time when job possibilities can be reviewed and career ambitions discussed is during the annual appraisal. In my experience, and that of millions of managers around the world, very often the appraisal or performance review is a painful paper-filling tick-box exercise hated by line managers and employees alike. Too often the 'conversations' (and I do use that term loosely) involve the line manager telling the employee whether they have or haven't hit their targets, and then setting targets for the next year. Occasionally, there might be a brief discussion regarding the Personal Development Plan, if it is part of the form, but it usually falls to the employee to fill in later. This doesn't aid performance, nor does it explore the true passions and desires of the employee being appraised. It does provide a reminder of the individual's targets, but to be honest, given how time-poor most managers are, it probably would have been more effective if these were by email. Of course, going through the motions of the exercise does get HR off your back, and the organization feels better about the fact that they are managing the performance of their employees. It is all slightly depressing, isn't it, and a complete waste of everyone's time and energy.

What would happen to conversations between manager and employee if they started the performance review with the question "When was the last time you caught yourself doing something that you love?" That would change the dynamic of the performance review meeting completely. Just consider what could happen if managers and employees explored this question with honesty and transparency. For a start, a conversation that begins with a question that requires reflection and touches on someone's values and beliefs is richer and more profound than one based on a paper exercise. Secondly, it also forces you to drop out of task mode for a time and focus on the person, who they are, what they are, what they are capable of, examining their potential and their passions. The review meeting would discover a whole range of possibilities for the employee to improve their performance and add value to the organization. Wow! All from a simple question about stuff they love to do.

How does such a conversation help a line manager? Connecting on a deeper level helps you to understand what makes the employee tick and where their passions might help the team. Some might have a passion for numbers and analyzing data, others for meeting people. Talking about what they love will enable you to understand the types of projects and job tasks that they would embrace and enthuse about. You might also discover that these people who come to work day in and day out spend their spare time coaching kids' football teams, organizing charity events, or volunteering for a counseling helpline, demonstrating a whole heap of transferable skills that these individuals might never have had the opportunity to use in the workplace.

The reward for the organization of such an approach to performance and development reviews is immense. Engagement is such an overused word, but if people are doing what they love, engagement isn't something that has to be strived for, it will be a given. The organization will be filled with an employee population doing what they love at least some of the time, delivering a significant level of discretionary behavior, and creating an atmosphere that makes the organization a great place to work and that results in great organizational performance and high levels of profit.

Manage Your Career Tool #7 – What Does Success Mean to You?

Very often, we go through life with vague notions of what success looks like and pursue a set of goals that we believe will make us happy. But, very rarely, do we sit back and take time to stop and consider whether the goals we are pursuing are really the ones that will make us happy, and whether what we think makes us successful will really make us happy. This Career Tool provides an opportunity for you to take stock of what really matters to you, and helps you to define what success is, for you. The tool comprises three tasks:

- What does success mean to you?
- How other people define success?
- How you define success?

One thing to consider when you write your definition is whether what you have written is in your capacity to achieve. If your definition of success is based on how someone else behaves or acts, then you might be better served throwing pennies into a wishing well. Success measures are about you and what makes you feel successful, not about how other people feel about you.

Task 1 – What Does Success Mean to You?

Write a personal definition of success below:

_____

_____

_____

_____

_____

_____

_____

_____

_____

_____

_____

_____

_____

_____

_____

Task 2 – How Other People Define Success?

Success has been defined by a number of people in a number of ways. Below are some quotes. Read through each quote and circle key words that you believe are important to defining success. If any of these quotes are particularly powerful, highlight the whole quote:

- My favorite definition of success is that it is a state of mind combined with a state of readiness. You can have one and be a flop; if you have both, you'll win every time.—Carolyn Warner
- Put your heart, mind, intellect and soul into even your smallest acts. This is the secret of success.—Swami Sivananda
- If there is any one secret of success, it lies in the ability to get the other person's point of view and see things from his angle as well as your own.—Henry Ford
- Success is the sum of small efforts, repeated day in and day out.—Robert Collier
- There are no secrets to success. It is the result of preparation, hard work, learning from failure.—Colin Powell
- The major difference I've found between the highly successful and the least successful is that the highly successful stick to it. They have staying power. Everybody fails. Everybody takes his knocks, but the highly successful keep coming back.—Sherry Lansing, Chairman, Paramount Pictures
- Passion is what gives meaning to our lives. It's what allows us to achieve success beyond our wildest imagination. Try to find a career path that you have a passion for.—Henry Samueli
- To laugh often and much; to win the respect of intelligent people and the affection of children; to earn the appreciation of honest critics and endure the betrayal of false friends; to appreciate beauty; to find the best in others; to leave the world a bit better, whether by a healthy child, a garden patch, or a redeemed social condition; to know even one life has breathed easier because you have lived. This is to have succeeded.—Ralph Waldo Emerson

- You never achieve success unless you like what you are doing. —Dale Carnegie
- Success means only doing what you do well, letting someone else do the rest.—Goldstein S. Truism
- The measure of success is not whether you have a tough problem to deal with, but whether it's the same problem you had last year. —John Foster Dulles
- Success is how high you bounce when you hit bottom.—George S. Patton
- Our business in life is not to get ahead of others, but to get ahead of ourselves—to break our own records, to outstrip our yesterday by our today.—Stewart B. Johnson
- Be there for others, but never leave yourself behind.— Dodinsky
- Success is not the key to happiness. Happiness is the key to success. If you love what you are doing, you will be successful.—Albert Schweitzer
- Success is not counted by how high you have climbed but by how many people you brought with you.—Wil Ros
- Success is a journey, not a destination. The doing is often more important than the outcome.—Arthur Ashe
- Money won't create success, the freedom to make it will.—Nelson Mandela

Take up one idea. Make that one idea your life—think of it, dream of it, live on that idea. Let the brain, muscles, nerves, every part of your body be full of that idea, and just leave every other idea alone. This is the way to success.

What are the common themes of success that you have noted in the above quotations?

_____

_____

_____

_____

If you highlighted a particular quote, why did you chose it as a favorite?

_____

_____

_____

_____

_____

Task 3 – How You Define Success?

Most people seek to be a 'success.' Yet few have given great thought to what they mean by the term. In a letter written to the other people, offer your personal definition of success. As well as giving an overall personal definition of success, include at least one specific way you wish to experience career success. Use some of the themes and words that you identified in Task 2 to help you

_____

_____

_____

_____

_____

_____

_____

_____

_____

_____

_____

CHAPTER 7

Do the Important Stuff First

Because, as we all know, it's easier to do trivial things that are urgent than it is to do important things that are not urgent, like thinking. And it's also easier to do little things we know we can do than to start on big things that we're not so sure about.

—John Cleese

When we hear about the early death of a celebrity, whether that be Anton Yelchin, Paul Walker, or Heath Ledger, we discuss the wasted talent caused by the use of drugs or alcohol that side-tracked fantastical talent and stopped the individual from expressing their talent to its fullest. But talent isn't restricted to the greats or to celebrities, and wasted talent happens daily in organizational life. For many individuals, they do a job because they have bills to pay. It may be that they fell into a job because it was the only one they could get at the time, and this has led to a career path they are following not because it is an expression of who they are, or because it utilizes their talent, but just because that is the opportunity that has presented itself. For others, they may have believed their teachers, parents, or bullies at school when they were told they would never amount to anything, and lost their confidence in any talent that they did have. Alternatively, individuals may not have had the opportunity to understand what their talent is or not had a lucky moment when they fully realize what it is they are good at, so spend their whole lives believing that they don't have a purpose, deserve nothing better, and worse still that they are useless.

In our early years, our measure of success and capability is linked to our educational achievements, and how we measure up against our peers in class tests and exams becomes a defining part of our childhood. Education, often seen as an essential part of freedom and an enabler for freeing people to succeed in life, has moved away from helping children to succeed in whatever area of life they have a talent for, and has, through a process of managerialism switched the emphasis to rankings and qualifications. More and more pressure is put on children at an early age to reach a specified standardized score in a narrow band of subjects but specifically in reading, writing, and mathematics. Our success as children is limited to those individuals who have academic talent, at the detriment of those who are creative, artistic, or sporty. We, therefore, learn at an earlier age that we don't have talent or lack ability because we fail to meet the criteria that we are being measured by.

But talent doesn't necessarily equate to academic achievement; just look at Virgin Boss, Richard Branson, who had no exams and left school early, and yet have an amazing talent as an entrepreneur and leader. Childhood measures of talent are limited to just a few types of talent or intelligence. Being able to be a success in life takes more than being able to answer a math question, or answer a comprehension question about a set text that you have read. Human intelligence is much more complex than that and has so much more to offer, than being good academically, and yet this is the yardstick by which we measure our children and condition beliefs about talent. Gardener (1983) identified nine types of intelligence:

1. Spatial: visualizing the world in 3D
2. Naturalist: understanding living things and reading nature
3. Musical: discerning sounds, their pitch, tone, rhythm, and timbre
4. Logical–mathematical: quantifying things, making hypotheses, and proving them
5. Existential: tackling the questions of why we live and why we die
6. Interpersonal: sensing people's feelings and motives
7. Bodily–kinesthetic: coordinating your mind with your body
8. Linguistic: finding the right words to express what you mean
9. Intrapersonal: understanding yourself, what you feel and what you want

Gardener (1983) offers a much more holistic approach to human capacity and his model challenges set notions of what it is to be talented, providing a much richer kaleidoscope of what it is that makes individuals successful and able. Many people go through their whole lives not realizing their talent, and many would read a book like this and believe that they don't have talent, and that this chapter doesn't apply to them. To those people I say it is time to recognize the talent you possess. Everyone, and I mean everyone, and that includes you, has talent. There, I said it. Now just to reiterate, to make sure you got the message—EVERYONE including YOU has talent.

Finding Talent

So, now we have established that you have talent, the question is, what is it and, more importantly, how do you find it? Firstly, the talent you possess will be unique to you but this doesn't necessarily mean it will be valued by the world at large. I don't say this to depress you, but for you to understand that your talent has value in specific places. It might be that your talent will lead you to receive a Nobel Peace Trump, but it might not lead to worldwide recognition and fame. It could be that you win a Grammy or that you just make kids smile in the school gym. Talent comes in all shapes and sizes, and it also isn't always recognized the way it should be. It's why talent shows like Britain's Got Talent are so popular, there's always a Susan Boyle out there who can get Simon Cowell to raise his eyebrows in surprise. We don't all get the recognition we deserve, but it doesn't mean that we don't possess some awesome talent. Also some types of talent lead to red carpets, others lead to a life of service, without a Golden statue. For example, in most organizations, there exists the most fantastically talented administrator. The person who makes sure that the stationary cupboard is always stocked, who actually balances the various elements that ensure that a department runs smoothly. They are the unsung heroes of an organization and are only appreciated when they leave a business or go on holiday for two weeks and the whole place goes to pot. These people might not ever get international acclaim for their efforts, but they have a talent that, even if it is not recognized, adds enormous value to an organization and to the people who work in it.

Secondly, your talent might be significant only in particular situations and contexts. By this I mean that your talent is only talented in certain circumstances. For example, David Beckham's ability to calculate the angle and distance of kicking a football in order to bend it like Beckham is only useful on a football field. In a sales office, Beckham would be a failure, but as a football professional, his talent was lauded. The moral of the story is that your talent might not be appreciated in the context in which you find yourself. It might be that you have an amazing talent that is not utilized in your current situation. Maybe you will need to change where you are, for your talent to be recognized and put to good use.

Thirdly, your talent will probably seem ordinary to you. It usually is something you are good at naturally. Whether that is your ability to find your way around an engine or an IT system, the mysterious way you connect and network with people without realizing it, how you can work out the logical steps needed to solve a problem without effort, or solve impossible interpersonal problems bringing a calming presence and bringing people together and collaborating seamlessly. Most people only realize they have a talent when someone else spots it or asks you to break down what you have just done and you can't because it's just something you can do. Therefore, become aware of the stuff that people ask you to do because you are good at it. Notice the things that you can just do without effort, and have somehow found yourself as the 'go to person' for a particular thing. Don't just rely on your own intuition about what might be your area of talent; ask colleagues, family, and friends what they think your strengths are. You might discover a theme of strengths you possess that maybe you weren't even aware of but that are appreciated by those around you.

Finally, talent only becomes useful when it is developed. Raw talent is exceptional, and we all have talent in a raw form. But like anything, it can only be utilized when we understand how to tap into it, how to use it properly and appropriately, and when we understand how to use it fully. Syed (2010) in his book, Bounce, observed that talent came from 10,000 hours of purposeful practice and expert talent comes from knowledge. Being good at something will only take you so far; talent, fully realized can only be utilized when you work hard to develop it, understand it, and take time to refine it. For example, the television in our lounge has a remote control, which has about eighty buttons on it. I can use the on/off button, the channel changing buttons, the volume buttons, and the button to switch from TV to DVD, about ten percent of the capacity of the remote control. There is nothing wrong with that, because I can use the buttons I need to operate the TV. It performs the function it is designed for, but it does mean that I don't fully understand or have the ability to fully capitalize on the total capability of our TV. For all I know it might be able to make me a cup of tea and order my weekly shopping. You laugh, but how would I know what is possible without understanding how it works?

Using this analogy, consider your talent; currently, you may only be aware of some of its most basic functions, which in itself makes you better than the next person at what you are doing. However, if you are only using ten percent of your full talent capability, then you are not yet capitalizing on your full potential, you are simply scratching the surface.

How Much Talent Potential Do You Have?

Your successful utilization of your talent potential will only become known as you stretch the boundaries of what you think you are capable of. Therefore, take every opportunity you have to understand and develop your talent. A 10,000 hours might seem like an impossible amount of time to dedicate to become excellent; however, you have a lifetime to find out what you are really capable of, so there is every chance that this goal is within your reach.

In truth, no one knows what he or she is truly capable of until they try. How can we know what abilities we were born with until we are given an opportunity to do something with them? Sometimes, the only way we can discover whether we can do something is to be brave enough to give it a go. More importantly, we must not allow ourselves to settle for a comfortable level of achievement, when it comes to our talent. We must continue to invest in our talent in order to continuously improve; it is always possible to go one better. If we don't invest in our talent, especially in developing our skills and knowledge, then we begin to get stagnant. There appears to be a perception that as you age, you become an 'old hat'—but this perception is misconceived. We only become outdated when we stop learning and developing ourselves. The moment we begin to believe that we no longer need to develop our skills, knowledge or behaviour, is the moment that our talent begins to decline. The world continues to move forward. What was good today will not be good enough tomorrow, and, therefore, we need to work hard to stay relevant and keep our talent fresh. Potential is elusive, it is something yet to be determined, an opportunity to be discovered at a later date. We do not yet know what we are truly capable of. Don't let others prevent you from living to your full potential. Stop making excuses and start living your talent.

Whatever your future capability, do the important stuff now:

- Value your own talent, because it might not be recognized by other people.
- Realize that your context defines whether your skills, knowledge, and capability are recognized and valued.
- Your ordinary is someone else's extraordinary; recognize your extraordinary for yourself.
- Be deliberate about developing your talent; keep pushing yourself to get better.

Manage Your Career Tool #8 – What Can You Own?

Very often, we will make excuses for why we can't do something, blaming inexplicable forces that get in the way of our ability to get on with getting on. However, many of the barriers that we face turn out to be little more than assumptions about what we can or can't do.

Clive Woodward in his book, Winning, describes how he worked with the England Rugby team, leading them to victory in the 2003 Rugby World Cup. In the book, he describes his determination to bring as much as possible under his control in order to support the team in achieving success. There were things that the coaching team couldn't do anything about (ICDFAA); these we things like the weather, the time that the rugby matches were to be played, or the condition of the pitch. There were things that the team could influence (ICI). This included persuading the rugby teams that the international players played for, to release the players to make them available for a summer training camp, or to ensure that the team would get time to acclimatize to the heat in Australia. Finally, there were those things that the team could take ownership for (ICO); nutrition, training regimes, fitness, and physiotherapy. The team worked hard to bring as much stuff into their sphere of ownership as possible, and where they couldn't own it, recognizing who and what they could bring under their sphere of influence.

The same principles can be used in developing your talent. This means identifying what you can own, what you can influence and what you can, quite frankly, do nothing about. In Task 1, you need to consider your career and your talent development, keeping mind the 10,000 hours of purpose practice required to release your talent potential and develop your expertise. Once you have completed the task, take the actions required to begin the process of owning the release of your talent potential.

Task 1 – I Can Own, I Can Influence, I Can't Do Anything About

Complete the table below giving consideration to your career and your talent development, keeping mind the 10,000 hours of purpose practice required to release your talent potential and develop your expertise. Identify what you can own, what you can influence and what you can do nothing about.

ICO	ICI	ICDFAA

CHAPTER 8

What You Are and What You Are Not

The most common way people give up their power is by thinking they don't have any.

—Alice Walker

If you're rich, it is obvious that you are not poor; if you are happy, you are not sad; if you are patient, you are not impatient. You don't need to read a book to understand the obvious. My biggest what I am not is that I am not patient; I am impatient, so far, so obvious. I have always struggled with the fact that I am not patient and have tried to learn patience. But, even when I am trying to be patient, I am like a kid trying to sit still— I end up wiggling around. I end up saying things like "I know I should be more patient about this but . . .". Being impatient is really annoying. Why can't I just wait serenely, in a place of peace and calm, rather than find myself getting frustrated by the lack of progress? To make matters worse, I am a visionary, I think big, and have big ideas about what could be. Achieving my dreams takes time, they don't just happen overnight. The relief when I achieve a dream isn't so much relief that I've achieved my dream, but a relief from the frustration of wishing I had already achieved it. For a brief period I experience peace, until I start thinking big again and the process of impatient frustration begins once more. Sometimes, the time it takes to achieve something is a LONG time for someone who is impatient. Most of the time the impatience thrums away and I can ignore it, but every now and again, the din gets louder and I go through a period where I admonish myself for not being patient enough. "It will happen" I tell myself. "When?" Comes next. "Soon" is the reply. "How soon is soon?" I lament. I'm like the kid in the back of the car asking "Are we there yet?" But no matter how many times I go through the periods of impatience, I keep going. During the impatient period, I bemoan the issues and problems I am facing and want to quit the journey.

But, despite my complaints, I won't give up. I can't give up. This is because I am Tenacious. I will stick at it if I believe that I am doing the right things, and that if I keep doing the right things eventually I will get there. I won't quit, no matter how frustrated I get. I will continue to journey on, in pursuit of my vision. But I am what I am not. My tenacity makes me impatient. I am tenacious, therefore, I am not patient. I could not continue forward, overcoming obstacles and continue believing that I have a future and a hope if I was patient. It's not that if you are patient you can't pursue dreams and persevere; tenacity is about holding fast. So, you can be tenacious and patient. But my tenacity is not about holding fast. My tenacity is related to the fact that I will not relinquish or let go of the pursuit of the vision I have, because I cannot stop pursuing my vision I cannot be patient in the sense of waiting. I have realized that the sense of relief and calm I feel on achieving a dream is in the ending of the pursuit rather than the achievement of the dream itself. It is my tenacity that fuels my energy to continue on even when I get fed up and tired of the journey. So, rather than beat myself up for not being patient, I will instead celebrate the tenacity that makes me who I am, because it is that tenacity that makes me what I am not—I am not someone who has the patience to stop pursuing my dreams.

Embracing Your Weaknesses

I get frustrated when listening to managers working on personal development plans because the focus is on developing individual weaknesses rather than developing their strengths. In Career Tool #2, you were asked to focus on identifying your strengths and spending time thinking about your strengths is essential in understanding who you are. But, although I don't advocate developing areas of weaknesses beyond ensuring they don't get in the way of you playing your strengths, it doesn't mean that you should ignore your weaknesses altogether, or that recognizing your weaknesses doesn't have value. Weaknesses, viewed within the context of how they impact what you, are not a means that rather than castigating yourself for having weaknesses you begin to understand yourself in a holistic sense. You are who are you, not just because you have strength, but because your weaknesses also contribute to making you who you are too. A weakness may disadvantage you in specific situations or areas, but it may be advantageous in other circumstances. My impatience is advantageous because it drives me forward, it causes me to not quit, and stay the course. In some circumstances, it has a negative effective, but, in others, it provides me with a competitive advantage.

Clark (2014) suggests that we need to reframe our understanding of the totality of ourselves to understand that the mix of both our strengths and our weaknesses is a scarce resource, and rather than competing on someone else's terms, we should compete on our own playing field to gain clarity about what makes us special. This premise supports the idea that just as our strengths are part of our talent, so too are our weaknesses. Sometimes, those traits that we assume are negative are the very ones required for a particular situation, or combined with our strengths become a toxic combination that helps us achieve the extraordinary. The dogged single mindedness of Einstein was frustrating and led to him breaking with more social conventions and rules than was acceptable; at the same time, his rule-breaking led to him making huge leaps in the field of physics. If he hadn't been so singular in his approach, in all likelihood, we would never have heard his name. In understanding that our weaknesses can complement or even enhance our strengths, we can begin to grasp the fullness of who we are, and what exactly it is we can bring to the party.

What We Assume Are Our Weaknesses, Are Merely Minor Strengths

I often hear development clients tell me "I am not . . ." yet on further exploration, I find out that they do in fact possess the qualities they tell me that they don't have. Often the "I am not" comes from a false perception of the quality that they believe they don't have, or have been told incorrectly over many years by others that they don't hold these qualities. Take the quality of 'creativity' as an example. The number of individuals I encounter who believe they are not creative is huge; you might be one of them. This is because they believe that creativity is artistic or out there and requires the need to be colorful, extravagant, and about new invention. However, creativity isn't the same as new invention. It can be inventive, but it is also about imagination or being able to create differently. If we were to study the Dyson vacuum cleaner, we would say that James Dyson is an inventor. I think we would agree that the Dyson was inventive and creative in tackling the problem of suction in vacuum cleaners, which changed the dusty (pun intended) vacuum cleaner market and shaking things up with cyclone technology. But vacuum cleaners aren't new, and neither was cyclone technology. Dyson's creativity was in combining the two. Or take the iPod. A fabulous piece of engineering inventiveness, which shook the foundations of the music market and forever changed the way we access and interact with music. If we look at the history of portable music, before MP3 players began to surface we had the delights of the Boombox, Sony Walkman, followed by the CD Discman, and finally the iPod. However, the iPod simply took the idea of digital and portable music, added the Apple design credentials, and put thought into where the music downloads would come from. The real invention wasn't the iPod but the digital music download market, and before you knew it, the music industry was changed forever. These advances were creative, inventive, but based upon what had already gone before. In many ways their invention evolved from previous ideas, products, and services. So what does it mean to be creative? If you use your passenger seat as desktop, wedge a door open with a piece of paper or develop a makeshift seat out of box, that is creativity. Not all creativity has to be iPod level creativity; it is simply using your imagination to create something.

Very often we mistake the extremes of a capability as being the only way a quality can be included in our arsenal of abilities without realizing that there are different levels and applications of qualities in much the same way as the continuum between mega creativity from apple to using a box as a chair. Take my weakness of impatience, for example. Patience can be viewed as someone sitting serenely waiting, calm, and biding his or her time, unflustered and unshaken. I am not like that. But if you look at what patience is, although it can mean calm, it also means tolerant perseverance or forbearance and, in this respect, I am patient. I might get frustrated and have internal conversations ranting about the situation. But I keep on going, believing that it will happen eventually. I don't give up, and I don't quit just because things aren't going the way I want them to. You might have a whole list of hang ups about not being good something, when, in reality, you are comparing yourself with a standard, which is not realistic. You might not be great at writing a report, if the person you are comparing yourself with has an extreme talent in that area, but it doesn't mean that you are not GREAT, just not AS great. It is a matter of degrees rather than absolutes.

Not Everything You Believe About Yourself Is True

Growing up, I was told repeatedly that I was selfish, and so I believed that I was not generous until I was confronted with a ream of evidence to the contrary. I don't say this to blow my own trumpet, but to illustrate how lies fed into us as children can stay with us throughout our adulthood, making us doubt our true character and capability. Now that I am a parent, I realize how literally words can be taken, even when they are not meant in that way. We can falsely believe something about ourselves, assume that we have this terrible weakness that is disabling, when in fact, it is a miscommunication that happened at a singular point in time, that has led us to believe something that is patently not true. These false beliefs are probably the most insidious aspect of developmental stagnation. Thinking that we can't or that we don't or that we are in absolutist terms is extremely dangerous. In a world which is full of gray edges, where in so many areas that are any definitive black or white answers only degrees of being, absolute thinking is exceptionally problematic.

It is important, therefore, that you spend time considering all things you are not and taking time to revisit them to discover how much more like those things you really are. You might just find out that you are in fact more passionate, compassionate, vocal, organized, creative, patient, generous, visionary, strong, daring, and amazing than you believed you were. The truth is we are all more than we let ourselves believe.

Manage Your Career Tool #9 – Owning Your Weaknesses

Adapted from (Buckingham, 2010)

The process for identifying your weaknesses is the same as identifying your strengths, only this time you will be using the list your capture in the dislike column in Career Tool #2. The next step is to articulate your weaknesses. There are 2 tasks to do this:

1. Articulate weaknesses
2. Write a weakness statement

Writing a weakness statement, like that of a strengths statement can be time consuming, but it is important that you examine what your perceived weaknesses are. Once these are articulated, you are able to decide whether these weaknesses should be embraced because you are not what you are not, whether they are just minor strengths or actually some of the weaknesses you identified need to be challenged because they are in fact not true. Like identifying strengths, owning weaknesses is not a one-time activity. As you develop your career, you will discover more weaknesses or reveal more insecurities as you improve your self-awareness.

Task 1 – Articulate Weaknesses

Having identified those activities that you disliked in Career Tool #2 Task 1, consider how it is those activities make you feel ineffective. Rewrite the tasks listed in the disliked column to make it identifiable as a weakness

For example, I feel weak when I create tutor resources.

_____

_____

_____

_____

_____

_____

_____

_____

_____

_____

_____

_____

_____

_____

_____

Task 2 – Write a 'Weakness Statement'

To develop a weakness statement, take "the verb (the doing word) and then drill down into what context you feel most [weak] in." (Buckingham, 2010)

For example, I feel weak when creating tutor resources because I find it painful working within the constraints of imposed templates and structure. I find that being creative within a structure interrupts my creative flow and feels forced.

_____

_____

_____

_____

_____

_____

_____

_____

_____

_____

_____

_____

_____

CHAPTER 9

Challenge, Question, Be Curious

The important thing is not to stop questioning. Curiosity has its own reason for existing.

—Albert Einstein

Good development practice relies on asking good questions and, more importantly, asking the right questions. The same is true in all aspects of life. Whether it is the CEO asking the right questions of their team to get a picture of what is really going on; managers asking the right questions to get commitment from their team on the tasks that are being completed; employees asking the right questions of their managers to make sure that they understanding what they are really achieving in carrying out a task; or a trainer asking the right questions to understand the nub of the development issue. Questions are important for efficiency and effectiveness. They are powerful tools. Asking the right questions can engage and motivate the person being asked the question into action. Asking the wrong questions can lead to misunderstanding, wrong assumptions, and actions that take you in the wrong direction and asking an unreasonable question leads to answers that are unhelpful or which lack wisdom.

The Right Type of Question

In his book, A More Beautiful Question, Berger (2014) argues that, "one good question . . . can generate whole new fields of inquiry and can prompt changes in entrenched thinking. Answers, on the other hand, often end the process." The key to asking the right question is to be clear on the reason why you are asking the question in the first place. What is your intention? Knowing why you are asking questions will help you to choose your questions well. For example, when something goes wrong, you could ask:

1. Why does this keep happening?
2. What's wrong with you?
3. Why did you do that?

As soon as we ask these questions, our brains go to work, serving up automatic answers. The answers are part of our mental models, the way in which we filter information to reinforce our current view of the world. Rather than thinking around the problem, the questions reinforce the assumptions we have already made about why the problem happened. But ask different questions, and we can challenge our perspective. Mezirow (1991) describes perspective transformation as a situation where an individual is freed from their assumptions, which have been developed as a result of their upbringing. Good questions, correctly framed can cause you to become critically aware of how your current thinking is distorted a nd, as a result, may be impacting negatively on your problem solving and decision-making. As you engage in a process of critical reflection prompted by these questions, they have the ability to transform your frames of reference and develop new perspectives. If you don't confront your habits of mind and frames of reference through a process of critical reflection, learning cannot be transformative and you remain stuck in familiar patterns of thinking.

Berger (2014) suggests that there are three kinds of questions that are effective:

- **Why Questions** inspire innovation and give you a new perspective resulting in new solutions being found when you refuse to accept the existing reality.
- **What if Questions** help to release you from what you think you already know, reveal possibilities, and open the door to the development of fresh approaches.

- **How Questions** enable you to test ideas to create new ways of doing things beyond what has been done before.

Questions enable us to traverse an increasing complex business environment, which demands new solutions to new problems and requires us to be purposeful in our endeavors. A good question, therefore, is essential if we are to prompt change, challenge the familiar, and create a curiosity for the new.

If You Think You Have All the Answers, You Haven't Asked All the Questions

Janis (1972) suggested that when a team makes a decision, it is possible that it can be impacted by a phenomenon called groupthink. This is where people engage in a negative cycle of decision-making, which is driven by a failure by the group as whole to test the reality upon which they are basing group decisions. The end result can be catastrophic where teams fail to weigh decisions properly and make false judgments based upon societal norms of moral judgment. Rather than challenging wrong-headed thinking, within a team, which has succumbed to groupthink, you may find yourself bowing to group pressure against your better judgment. In a particular situation or context, this may lead you to begin to rely on others to make important decisions without discussion or question. Teams who succumb to groupthink are prone to downplaying negative feedback, rewarding conformity, and suppressing unpopular ideas or information that contradicts the group's perceived truth. This links to the current issues with populist fake news stories, whereby individuals get all their information from the same source, and live in social media bubbles. If anyone questions the validity of claims by the group then the combative response from others will pressure an individual to stay on message. In the end, reason loses and challenge becomes dangerous. Our sources of information confirm what we already believe to be true, and when our version of the truth is under threat, we stop asking questions, but this limits our thinking and our ability to experience transformative learning.

As individuals, it is important that we challenge our thinking on a regular basis. Assuming that we know what we already know happens when we fail to ask questions. In order to remain curious, we must continue to ask questions to gain a more holistic understanding of a particular issue. For example, if you are asked "What's wrong with you?", there is an assumption by the person asking the question that the problem lies with you. In their mind, they may already have a list of possible answers. Maybe, it's because:

- You're too slow/quick to act.
- You're inexperienced/overqualified.
- You're too assertive/passive.

But what if, what is wrong is not you, but the behavior or actions taken by another person. Maybe, they are inexperienced and, as a result, you find their decision making flawed, given your own understanding. In a situation where someone is performing poorly, an assumption that you are too passive means that whatever the question that is asked, the answers you give will reinforce the assumptions made and provide an excuse for the person to ask the question to determine that your passivity is the reason why you are not delivering the results you should. But different questions would prompt different responses and bring clarity to the situation. For example, if someone is not performing you could ask:

1. How clear are you about what you were asked to do? Which introduces the possibility that there was miscommunication or a lack of communication in setting the task.
2. What are the two or three attributes that made you the best person to do the task I set? Which opens up the qualities that can enable the individual to successful achieve a task.
3. How can I follow-up in a way that makes it easier for you to ask for help? If the situation has changed, or the framing of the task doesn't fit the reality of the situation, this question creates a line of communication to reconfigure the task with the reality of the context.

4. How could my apparent liabilities really be an asset in this situation? As explored in Chapter 8, embracing our weaknesses makes us able to play our strengths.

These questions and others are constructive or are focused on appreciative inquiry (AI) empowering used to and new possibilities. They lead to action. And they will produce positive results. The last question is particularly challenging because it asks you to reveal those parts of you that we might be trying to hide. But, they can be an asset, for example, if you don't have enough experience, you aren't locked into the same assumptions as more experienced employees. It is easier for you to think outside a box you are not in and approach problems with a fresh perspective. There are four ways you can ask better, more empowering questions:

1. Become conscious of the questions you are asking.
2. Evaluate these questions: Is this a good question? If not, what's a better one?
3. Choose the better question; be intentional.
4. Consider the answers that are given in response to your questions; act on these insights.

Questions provide the key to unlocking our unlimited potential.
—Anthony Robbins

Manage Your Career Tool #10 – Seeking Success in Your Own System

David Cooperider said that, "we live in the world our questions create" (Adams, 2004). The AI is a method that uses questions to recognize the best of what is in people and is in the world around us. It is a process, which enables the participants to focus on strengths, successes, and our potential through the provision of a positive framework, using carefully crafted questions to help shape our perception. Although an AI process would typically take place over several days and be used in a group situation, appreciative questions are a useful tool for focusing your attention and enabling curiosity to set in motion creative and productive energy. This tool uses several appreciative questions to help you generate solutions and carry forward the best of your past and makes the optimal use of your current resources. There are four tasks for you to complete:

- Best experience
- Values
- Core life-giving factor or values.
- Three wishes

This tool seeks to help you explore you past and present capabilities and focuses attention on your achievements, strengths, opportunities, and unexplored potential to elevate your thoughts and harness your innovative thinking.

Task 1 – Best Experience

Tell a story about the best times that you have had in your career and personal development. Looking at your entire experience, recall a time when you felt most alive, most involved, or most excited about your involvement. What made it an exciting experience? Who was involved? Describe the event in detail. Recall a story about an exceptional empowering experience in your life. What made it remarkable?

_____

_____

_____

_____

_____

_____

_____

_____

_____

_____

_____

_____

_____

Task 2 – Values

What are the things you value deeply–specifically, the things you value about yourself, your family, your work, and your personal development?

_____

_____

_____

_____

_____

_____

_____

_____

_____

_____

_____

_____

_____

_____

Task 3 – Core Life-Giving Factor or Value

What do you think is the core life-giving factor or value of your career or personal development? What is it that, if it did not exist, would make your career or personal development totally different than it currently is?

_____

_____

_____

_____

_____

_____

_____

_____

_____

_____

_____

_____

_____

_____

Task 4 – Three Wishes

If you had three wishes for your career or personal development, what would they be?

_____

_____

_____

_____

_____

_____

_____

_____

_____

_____

_____

_____

_____

_____

CHAPTER 10

Make Yourself Heard

I just want my career to be run a certain way. When you get the sense it's not, that your voice is not being heard, then, unfortunately, you have to do certain things to make a stand to fight what you believe in, even if you do have to sacrifice time.

—Andre Ward

Ask any manager of any organization as to what gets in the way of performance and organizational effectiveness and in the top five will be communication. Investigate the artifacts of communication and you will notice that there is a lot of communication going on in the business and between individuals; meetings, presentations, newsletters, e-mails, phone calls, internal and external marketing campaigns, and memos. The issue is not so much the lack of communication in the organization, but the lack of appreciation that dialogue and discussion are dynamic processes. Communication isn't something that is a task to be completed, but is a continuous process, which should be used to build and strengthen relationships throughout the business. That dynamism can be used to bridge gaps, resolve conflicts, spark creativity, invite innovation, solve problems, and inspire collaboration.

Dialogue and discussion processes provide the foundation to create opportunities for people to engage with the organization and with each other, and it is this engagement that is the powerhouse behind developing the adaptable and flexible capability required for sustainable individual and organizational performance. Dialogue is different from exchanging one-way communication messages. It is a process that requires the sharing of perspectives, experience, issues, and opportunities. It isn't about who is right, or who is wrong. It is not about judgment or decision-making, but rather about understanding and learning, which, in turn, helps the change-management process. Too often in our personal and organizational communication, whether an e-mail, report, or a presentation, the aim is not to be in dialogue with someone but to complete a task; we are broadcasting rather than exchanging, sending a message rather than listening.

Dialogue Improves the Decision-Making Process

There is a mistaken assumption that if you open up dialogue and invite participation, nothing will get done. However, if change is to take place, existing mental models need to be put to one side, a growth mind set needs to take center stage, and people need to be open to different perspectives that may be very different from their own. But, I hear you cry, decisions do still need to be made. Dialogue is what will help to shape the discussion that, in turn, will enable everyone to have their voices heard. Different viewpoints can be debated to tackle issues and conflicts in a new way, which isn't restricted by interpersonal or political influences. It isn't the case that inviting dissenting voices leads to disharmony, instead it creates a space for people to come together, and share in the decision-making processes. In the long term, it can reduce resistance and conflict, enhance relationships, develop agility, and improve the decision-making process. Engaging people to interact in the process of dialogue positively is a skill that can be learned, and one that is essential to ensure that issues can be moved forward and individuals with their own problems and issues can come together to find common ground.

There are five stages to fostering dynamic dialogue and discussion in your organization:

1. Get to know the issues and the stakeholders.
2. Establish ground rules and agreements regarding the dialogue and discussion process.
3. Share personal stories and perspectives enquiring about 'how' the issue affects each participant rather than focusing on solving the problem with a 'what should be done' approach.

4. Explore ALL views, listening, reasoning, and being thoughtful about how the participants can act together.
5. Decide upon next steps and make recommendations on how to implement the output of the discussion.

The key to dynamic dialogue and discussion is to create a space where the collective wisdom of the concerned stakeholders can be transformed into achievable decisions founded on agreed common ground. Everyone involved in the dialogue needs to take ownership for the process and the end result, as such everyone has a role to play and must add their voice to the situation. As explored in Chapter 9, questions are the key to great dialogue, alongside which all parties involved must be willing to work toward goals, which are mutually beneficial. There are a number of questions that are beneficial to a dialogue group aimed at focusing attention on developing an ongoing process of participative exchange. For example:

• What question could I ask that would make the most difference to this situation, now and in the future?
• What is it about this situation that makes it important to you and why do you care about the decisions that are made about it?
• What is our intention in finding an outcome? What is the real purpose that makes this the outcomes of dialogue worthwhile?
• What do we already know? What do we still need to learn?
• What are the opportunities and dilemmas about this situation, which affect the way we will make a decision about what action to take?
• What assumptions are we making? How can we test those assumptions to ensure our perception is aligned with fact?
• What would someone, who has a different belief say about this situation?

While we are in dialogue with other people, it is essential that we play our part in creating a positive environment in which discussion can flow. This means that we need to listen to what others say, being present in the moment, and not simply waiting for a pause in breath before we dive in with our thoughts and ideas. Listen to the words, watch body language, and try to understand the perspective being shared, even if you disagree with it. Take stock of what the interests and aspirations are of the people you are in dialogue with, even if you fundamentally disagree with what they represent, take time to understand what motivations, fears, concerns, and hope lie behind their position; in all likelihood, they are the same as yours. Also focus on the positives, the areas where you do agree, where there is common cause, and where action can be taken. As explored in Career Tool #11, focus on what you can own and influence instead of worrying about what you cannot do anything about.

Manage Your Career Tool #11 – Daily Temperature Reading

Adapted from Satir (1972)

The Daily Temperature Reading (DTR) was developed by Virginia Satir (1978) as a way of helping people communicate in a clear and effective way. Although the DTR model was developed to help families and partners, it is an especially helpful framework to use with colleagues at work to drive dynamic dialogue and discussion. The model introduces five areas, which it suggests should be kept current and alive between individuals in a relationship.

1. Appreciations
2. New information
3. Puzzles
4. Complaints and recommendations
5. Wishes, hopes, and dreams

The idea is that a DTR is done regularly to improve dialogue and discussion throughout the organization, and especially with individuals who have a project or work that rely on good communication. Sit down together and work through each of the five tasks in sequence. To begin with, the process and the dialogue might feel stilted and awkward, but with practice, it becomes an important ritual in establishing honest dialogue between individuals.

Task 1 – Appreciation

Express appreciation for something that your colleague has done. Take this time to thank each other for how your actions and behavior have helped move the project or work forward, and also helped on a personal level.

_____

_____

_____

_____

_____

_____

_____

_____

_____

_____

_____

_____

_____

Task 2 – New Information

Share new information with your colleague or in the absence of information, some assumptions you may be working with. Tell your colleague something which lets them know your mood, for example, "I'm not looking forward to the reaction to the report we submitted," and your experience. Then listen to what your colleague has to share.

_____

_____

_____

_____

_____

_____

_____

_____

_____

_____

_____

_____

_____

_____

Task 3 – Puzzles

This segment provides an opportunity to ask about any aspect of the work or project that you don't understand. Take turns asking your colleague to explain something such as "Why were the sales figures down last week?" Or take the opportunity to voice a question about yourself: "I don't know why I find it so difficult to work with the Finance team." The DTR session may not provide you with the answer you are looking for, but it will provide your colleague with some insight into what is going on with you. It also gives them the opportunity to share any insight they may have about your current situation or experiences.

_____

_____

_____

_____

_____

_____

_____

_____

_____

_____

_____

_____

_____

Task 4 – Complaint, with a Request for Change

This stage is not about placing blame or passing judgment. Instead provide insight into a specific behavior that bothers you and state the behavior you are asking for instead. "If you're not going to be able to prepare for a meeting, please call me. That way I can make a decision about whether the meeting needs to go ahead or whether it needs to be postponed to give you time to collate the information and avoid a situation where no decisions can be made."

_____

_____

_____

_____

_____

_____

_____

_____

_____

_____

_____

_____

_____

_____

Task 5 – Hopes

Sharing hopes and dreams is integral to a relationship. Hopes can range from the mundane "I hope you don't miss your train" to the grandiose "I'd really love it if we manage to get sign off for the new office building". The purpose of this segment is that you will all bring dreams into immediate awareness and in doing so creating an environment where you are the more likely to find a way to realize them.

_____

_____

_____

_____

_____

_____

_____

_____

_____

_____

_____

_____

_____

_____

CHAPTER 11

Dream Big

It's not about how to achieve your dreams, it's about how to lead your life . . . If you lead your life the right way, the karma will take care of itself, the dreams will come to you.

—Randy Pausch

How often do you daydream? You know those moments when you slip into a temporary state of imagining. Maybe you have had daydreaming beaten out of you when you were growing up. Certainly there is a huge amount of negativity about daydreaming whether as a child or an adult. Did you know that ten minutes of every hour you fall into Alpha state— or as you might think of it, zoning out, away with the fairies or daydreaming? Alpha state (Berger, 1940) involves the conscious mind turning inwards, transporting your mind to a different time and space.

You might think that this never happens to you, but have you ever come around when driving, having zoned out, not quite sure what junction you are up to on the motorway? You have passed dozens of vehicles, possibly gone through numerous maneuvers, but have no conscious memory of how you got where you are. In the USA, the traffic cops even refer to a 'black and white' syndrome, which occurs when someone who is driving perfectly safely in Alpha state suddenly becomes aware (conscious) of the police car and switches back to conscious thinking. The end result is rather than driving more safely, the driver begins driving erratically because they become overtly conscious of their actions.

Or consider this, when you walk up a flight of stairs, the first few steps you think about as you get a measure of the height and width of the stairs. Next time you ascend or descend a flight of stair, count how many stairs it takes before you stop thinking about walking up the stairs,

you'll find yourself wobbling more than usual, because the act of count-
ing forces you to think about how you are walking up and down the
stairs. If you have ever wondered why the top step on a spiral staircase
in a castle is always slightly lower than all the other steps in the castle, it
is because even several hundred years ago the castle builders had worked
out that invading soldiers stopped thinking about where they were placing their feet on the stairs by the time they had run up hundreds of
steps. So, the crafty builders deliberately reduced the height of the final
step in order to cause the invading soldier to stumble. This gave the
defenders an opportunity to step out of a hidden door and bop them
over the head. Daydreaming, it seems, is not a modern phenomenon; it
is part of what makes us human.

The Importance of Daydreaming

Daydreaming is essential to our mental wellbeing; it is our download time
and if you prevent yourself from daydreaming, you will find that when
you do daydream you will do so for longer and with greater intensity.
You might believe that you have full control over whether you daydream
or not, but consider for a minute a meeting or workshop that you have
recently attended. In the morning, as a willing participant, you will have
consciously prevented yourself from drifting off. You will have diligently
shifted the position in your seat in you efforts to stay focused and pay
attention, even during the boring bits. You may have found yourself
participating in activities to help you stay focused; sitting up straight,
drinking coffee, and even writing notes to stay focused, especially if the
presenter was droning on a bit. After lunch, however, the struggle to
remain focused gets harder, and by 2pm to 3pm, you will have found
yourself zoning out for long stretches.

But daydreaming isn't an activity without merit or importance to
our personal development and wellbeing. The greatest thing about the
Alpha state is that it is the hot bed of creativity. Our conscious minds can
only hold onto about eight pieces of information at any one time. But
our subconscious is like a massive warehouse with every single piece of
knowledge, thought, experience, and idea you have gathered during your
lifetime stored and accessible to your imagination. When we daydream,

we open up access to all that material stored away like a giant library. As we daydream, our brain peruses the shelves picking up information in a seemingly random jumble and throwing them out for us to ponder on. The wealth of a lifetime of experience and knowledge just waiting for an opportunity for your subconscious to poke and pry, creating the possibility of a great idea.

Make Daydreaming Deliberate

In my development practice, I urge my clients to daily Take Ten@Ten. The idea behind the daily practice is to encourage people to take time out from task lists and action point and just stop and reflect for a brief period. Reflection plays a significant part in personal development and growth and is a major element of my development practice. Reflection is described "as a process [which] seems to lie somewhere around the notion of learning and thinking. We reflect in order to learn something, or we learn as a result of reflecting" (Moon, 2004). Literature describes reflective practices as a deliberate attempt on behalf of the individual to confront imperfect existing knowledge, which concludes with transformation in meaning (Peltier et al, 2005; Dewey, 1933; Schön, 1983). My own research, demonstrated that reflective writing adds value by improving agility and preparing you for change. Furthermore, it is a great tool for improving the speed and quality of decision-making.

If you allow yourself to daydream, taking ten minutes every now and again, you never know what might occur. You might just come up with the next big idea that will add millions of dollars to your organization's bottom line, you might just figure out the way to solve a problem you have been grappling with, or take advantage of an opportunity that you have been presented with.

Dream Bigger

While driving back to North Wales recently from a day trip to London, I found myself daydreaming about what might be. With a busy household and hectic work life, I value these quiet moments when I am alone in the car as an opportune time to allow myself to daydream about possibilities, what might be and what could be, in order to shape my plans and actions. There are several projects that I have been dreaming about for about ten years. I am closer to achieving these dreams than I was ten years ago, and these dreams have more shape and substance to them, more clarity than when I first pondered their possibility. But as yet, the dreams have not been achieved although things are in progress for them to become a reality.

The radio was on in the background and as I was daydreaming; the presenter said; "dream bigger." Maybe because I was engaged in dreaming dreams at the time, his voice resonated with my thoughts. Now, my dreams are not small fry; it's a large enterprise; but there it was, a challenge to my thinking, perhaps my dream was too small. At the time I chuckled to myself and for the rest of the journey, I must admit I was stumped; and several days later, the question still irked me. I was still pondering how I could dream bigger than I was dreaming, which for someone like me who likes to think big is not a problem I usually suffer from. This process meant that I was then forced to reflect on how I had suddenly found myself in a position where I was struggling to dream bigger. It forced some uncomfortable self-examination:

- Where had these limits to my dreams come from?
- What were the boundaries that I was imposing on my dream?
- What assumptions were driving these self-imposed boundaries?
- Where had these assumptions derived from?

This isn't the first time that I have discovered some self-imposed boundaries. Some years ago, I was talking to a friend about our dreams for remodeling our house and some of the painful choices we were faced with to make the project work for our family. My friend innocently asked me "Why don't you just move house?" It was a fair question, but it threw me. Why was moving house not in our framework? There are many things about our house that I love not least the location and the south-facing garden, but there were also lots of things, that at the time frustrated me. I regularly cursed the layout of the kitchen, I would inwardly groan every time I went to the bathroom, the lounge was too dingy, the conservatory needed replacing, and the front room was cold. Moving wasn't in the framework because I moved a lot growing up; the house I lived in represented permanency, it was home, and I had never had a place that I could call home. Further reflection resulted in me realizing that since I had lived in the house for the longest period that I have lived anywhere, my heart and head had no desire to leave to another house, and in fact, the house had become my home. However, this process of reflection forced me to confront many of my mental models about what a home was and also prioritize the things that were really important to me. Although the choice remained with remodeling the house, what the remodel looked like evolved into from solving some of the niggles to developing a dream for creating a 'forever home.'

In terms of my daydream on the drive home from London, there were many reasons why my big dream was too small and plenty of limits that I am putting on myself. Firstly, I know that I am limiting myself to the local area because of my desire to be where my home is. I've since upscaled my big dream to include national and even global reach. Secondly, I am living one big dream in regards to my business and writing, something that I thought was going to take years hasn't, and my dreaming hadn't caught up with the new reality that I am living. I realized that now is the time to dream in a new paradigm and allow myself to think beyond my current experience and understanding of what is possible, to dream about the impossible.

Dreaming the Impossible

For some people, it is difficult to understand why anyone would dream the impossible. After all, what is the point of the impossible, but for me, that is the point of dreaming. If you only dream about what is possible, you will be forever limited by your experience and your current situation. The impossible dreams take you outside of your comfort zone and into new territory. It was through dreaming of the impossible that electricity was invented, a man was put on the moon, the World Wide Web was developed, and we all ended up with smartphones. If mankind had limited our dreams to what is possible, we would still be hunter-gatherers and living in wooden huts. We are ALL capable of achieving the impossible, but too often we reduce and limit ourselves to our current circumstances. My encouragement to you is that it is time to break out and dream bigger.

Manage Your Career Tool #12 – Dream Big

Revisit you answer to the question in Career Tool #5 and prepare an opening statement, which articulates your big dream. Be courageous about what is significant to you and challenge yourself to go beyond you existing paradigm. There are six parts to the dream statement, which you need to consider. Be honest and answer each question in the fullest way possible. Don't hold back for fear of ridicule or disappoint. This is your Big Dream, there are no wrong answers.

Task 1 – Develop a Dream Statement

Complete your Big Dream statement using the table below:

Topic or theme of your dream . . . be specific	
My feelings . . . take ownership; it's your dream	
Why it matters . . . in the short term	
Why it matters . . . in the long term	
Maybe I . . . acknowledge the limitations you have placed upon your dream. Be honest and humble	

CHAPTER 12

Don't Be Afraid

Everybody is a genius. But if you judge a fish by its ability to climb a tree, it will live its whole life believing that it is stupid.

—Albert Einstein

We all take failure very personally. Whether a failure in a relationship, a failure to find employment, a failure to make a project work, or a failure to achieve a grade on a paper—Failure *feels* personal. But feelings aren't the same thing as truth. Failure is part of life, and it is a useful and healthy part of life. It might not feel like it at the time, but it is through failure that we improve and grow. It is through failure that we learn more than through success. We rarely learn from getting things right, even if them being right was a result of luck rather than design, and we were just lucky it didn't go wrong. So what does that mean? Failure helps us grow. Failure is THE key to growth. If you are failing often that is because the road you are traveling requires you to grow and not be superficial. The circumstances you are in require you to be resilient, to have deep roots like an oak tree, not weedy roots that can be easily pulled up.

If something goes right, we rarely sit down and count the cost of success and wonder whether it was worth it. But businesses and individuals usually count the cost of failure. Reflect for a moment the times in your life when you have learnt the most about yourself, about your strengths, about something that has been life defining. I am fairly certain that most of those moments were not where you were first crossing the finish line or where you were being awarded the gold star, but instead, you most life-defining moments were those in the midst of failure, when it didn't go your way. I once listened to Tim Smit, the founder of the Eden Project in the UK, explain that it is only on when your nose is so close to the brick wall that you feel you are going to hit it that you spot the slim sliver of light, the crack in the wall that allows you to move forward. Failure doesn't stop you from progressing. It might be messy and there may be consequences that you have to work through, but you don't stop moving forward because of it. Failure is a master teacher, and in a place of failure we become excellent students.

Failure Means You Are Looking for Opportunities

When I started my first business as a novice entrepreneur, a mentor told me that if I did not make any mistakes I was not doing enough. It seems like a weird piece of business advice to be told to make mistakes, but how else will I learn what works, and what doesn't work for my business. We learn early on, even before we leave kindergarten, that failure is something to be avoided and it is something we are taught through a process of cultural osmosis, a societal norm to divert from anything that leads to an unwanted outcome. These contrast sharply with our instincts as children, which are to give things a whirl; imagine what would happen if no one dared make a mistake as a toddler—how would we ever learn to walk, talk, or be independent if we didn't embrace failure as infants? But, as we grow older, we are taught that failure is something to be ashamed of, that it has bad consequences, and at an extreme level, something to be afraid of. Throwing caution to the wind is in some way irresponsible and threatening. Which is a shame because when failure comes, we are ill equipped to deal with it. Embracing failure, however, is an essential part of growing up. We must get to the point where we are secure enough in ourselves that we understand that we are not the failure when things don't work out, but by not trying to avoid failing and actively trying to learn from failure when it happens enables us to grow as a person, in wisdom and in understanding.

Failure Isn't Because We Chose the Bad Decision

Who can say whether a choice is good or bad? At the time of making a choice, you make the best choice you can based upon the information you have available at the time. I can't imagine when faced with a decision you stand there and go "Oh that decision is *really* bad I'll chose that option." In my mind, a decision becomes a mistake only that we have more information than we did at the time of making the decision, which renders the decision we made a poor choice. The only mistake you can really make is not to learn from your mistakes. Therefore, all those mistakes you've made, you've learnt from, so they weren't really mistakes, but rather opportunities for development. On the same point, we can sometimes feel that if a decision turns out to be a mistake that we have missed out on a future that we hoped for. What could have been isn't the same as what should have been. Did I want my life to include nearly losing our house and what seemed like years of financial troubles? No, but it has shaped my thinking, and given me perspective. It has rounded off my sharp edges and softened me. Did I want to fail in business? No, part of my identity has always been that of being a 'successful business woman,' but failure has helped make me less fearful, it has made me trust that I can operate without a plan, it has given me fortitude which means I can move forward even when it feels like the road is crumbling at my feet. It turns out that you are who you are meant to be *because* of those brick walls you hit, not despite of them. They make you, you. I am an author *because* my business failed. I am living in purposeful endeavor because of my brick walls. You may lose a potential opportunity, and failure means you might take a circular route to 'get there' but you'll also find (as I am now) that the experience that you gain through failure will speed things up at the right time, so when the time comes to fulfilling your purpose, things will happen really quickly.

You Might Be a Deluded Megalomaniac

I sometimes hear people who are experiencing failure get out the whip to flog themselves over how they put themselves in this position. You cannot put yourself in a position of failure. If you even think for a minute you can possibly control all the forces and factors that cause the wind to blow this way or that, then you are either beating yourself up unnecessarily or a deluded megalomaniac. Someone close to me died in a car crash because of eight factors, any one of which had been a millimeter one way, a second the other, or slightly different and he would be alive today. Is it his *fault* he died? No. It was just a combination of things that led to his death. Stuff happens. Your position is not simply because you did X or Y. It's because stuff happens. This isn't about abdicating responsibility. If you are caught speeding when driving a car, you shouldn't have been speeding, but equally, what control did you have about where the speed camera or cop car was. None. You got caught speeding not just because you thought you could get away with, but also because, on that day, you couldn't get with it, because the police decided on that day, on that road, in that moment to set up a speed trap. Learn from your part in what led to failure, but don't act like you are master of the universe and your current situation is entirely within your power. Our best efforts can succeed or fail, not simply because we are the best or fail to be our best but because life sometimes throws us lemons and you know what they say about what you do if life throws you lemons, you make lemonade.

Weighing the Likelihood of Failure

An HR Director once told me that he thought everyone should be sacked from a job at least twice. It teaches you humility but also tenacity, and once you've been sacked a couple of times and survived, you stop worrying about being sacked and can do your job fearlessly and without compromising your values. Quite often, when I develop people and we discuss the dreams for their lives, there is nervousness about pursuing what they are passionate about because it might not work out. It is at this point that I bring out the Dr. Pepper question—"What is the worst that can happen?" For the majority of people, the decisions we make are inconsequential. No one is going to die, the world is not going to end, and life will carry on. If the failure is going to leave you no worse off than you are now, then the choice to take the risk becomes negligible.

When I made the decision to become self-employed, I was nervous about the financial consequences of removing the security of a regular salary and what might happen if I didn't get enough work. I had to face the fear that we could lose everything, we might not be able to pay our bills, we might not be able to pay our mortgage, and eventually we might lose our house. But should the worst happen, my children were not going to be homeless, they would have food in their bellies, clothes on their backs and shoes on their feet. My husband would stand with me and my marriage was strong with good friends and family around us. So, in making the decision to give up the day job, the worst that could happen is that we would lose our material wealth. But, equally, should things work out I might spend my life doing a job that I love and represent who I am, fulfilled and happy. As it turns out, I have experienced both. No quite losing the house, but certainly going through a period of time when an eviction notice was weeks away from being served. Not knowing what we were going to feed the kids and certainly not earning enough. We nearly experienced the worst. It wasn't a great time, and I hope I never have to experience it again. But we survived, and came out of the process stronger, fitter, and better than we were going in. Today, I am living the dream; I have secure, regular work in the diary for the next eighteen months. My income is not only better, but it is more secure now, than it was when I was working in corporate life with a three-month notice period. If you fail, the failure is only for today; it is not forever. Walking through failure might take time, and it might be really tough, but you will walk past it. Keeping going, believing that it will turn out all right in the end is what makes us human and ultimately leads to success. Remember other people will relay to you their successes, the fruit of their failure. But we don't talk about the moments when it got hairy and when it didn't quite go according to plan. We are presented stories of success that they happened cleanly in line with a plan. But every success story has failure in its history. Therefore, I can only conclude that giving up on yourself, on the people around you, and on pursuing your dreams and purpose is the only real failure in life.

Manage Your Career Tool #13 – Reframing Failure

Bouncing back from failure doesn't have to be an anxiety-ridden process. Resilience is a skill that can be learnt, and will enable you to cope when things inevitably go wrong. Resilience enables you to have the courage to ask questions about yourself, even if doing so means having to face up to some difficult truths. It is having the ability to think in a situation to understand what is best for you while balancing the need to keep relationships healthy and knowing the difference between right and wrong. Resilience enables you to take hold of a problem, develop creative solutions, and be resourceful in implement plans to overcome, all while maintaining humor and integrity. Reframing failure requires resilience; it means:

- Being comfortable with being uncomfortable when reviewing difficult issues
- Not allowing failure to destroy our self-worth
- Dealing with the situation as best we can, in that moment
- Choosing to have power over our failure, by taking a step back and learning from it, failure

There are four tasks in this exercise:

- Identify mistakes
- Think about the negative results
- Think about the positive results
- Think about what you have learned

When completing this exercise, you may find that as you tackle some of the tasks it is challenging revisiting difficult situations. I encourage you to be brave and keep in mind what it means to be resilient. Get into the habit of learning from mistakes, that way you can build toward success.

Task 1 – Identify Mistakes

Think back to those moments in your life where you have experienced a situation where you have failed spectacularly. Choose those occasions where you really messed up. No one else has to see your response to what is written. This is just you, reviewing yourself. There is no judgment, so please be as honest as possible.

_____

_____

_____

_____

_____

_____

_____

_____

_____

_____

_____

_____

_____

_____

Task 2 – What Were the Negative Results?

For each of the failure occasions that you identified in Task 1, reflect on all the negative consequences that arose as a result of the situation. We are covering these first, because they are the things that we tend to focus on when we fail. In the space below, fill in the Negative Results.

_____

_____

_____

_____

_____

_____

_____

_____

_____

_____

_____

_____

_____

_____

_____

_____

Task 3 – What Were the Positive Results?

Now the tricky bit; for each experience of failure that you wrote down in Task 1, what were the positive results that came out of that experience? It may be that for some mistakes you struggle to think of anything good that came out of it, so perhaps consider how, in relation to your life in general, things changed for the better. Capture these Positive Results in the space below.

_____

_____

_____

_____

_____

_____

_____

_____

_____

_____

_____

_____

_____

_____

_____

_____

Task 4 – What Did You Learn?

Lastly, for each experience of failure you listed in Task 1, consider what it was that you may have learned from your experience. Did you demonstrate resilience, or did the experience develop your knowledge and understanding about a particular situation or person. Did the experience teach you to do something differently or better, the next time? What did the experience teach you about yourself? Write what you learned in the space below:

_____

_____

_____

_____

_____

_____

_____

_____

_____

_____

_____

_____

_____

_____

_____

_____

CHAPTER 13

Choose the Right Attitude and You Will Find the Aptitude

We cannot change our past . . . we cannot change the fact that people act in a certain way. We cannot change the inevitable. The only thing we can do is play on the one string we have, and that is our attitude . . . I am convinced that life is 10 percent what happens to me and 90 percent how I react to it. And so it is with you . . . We are in charge of our attitudes."

—Chuck Swindoll

Sometimes I find myself in the unfortunate circumstance of meeting people who are energy sappers. You know the people I am talking about, the ones who are sallow faced, sitting in the corner (usually wrapped in a winter coat, which they keep on during the whole meeting), and who always have some drama or other that means their life is difficult at the moment. They also have to explain all the difficulties that are in their life, "oh woe is me", to anyone who is in the vicinity whether that person wants to listen or not. Perhaps, if you have never encountered a person like this, you are the energy sapper! I recently encountered an energy sapper who attended one of the workshops I was facilitating, sitting hunched in the corner exuding their life sucking negativity. This person had recently had an accident and, of course, the workshop provided the perfect opportunity to tell everyone all the awful dramas that occupied their life and the accident 'on top of everything else' gave further cause for seeking sympathy. At the end of the session, I was approached by the energy sapper with a view to bringing me up to speed on all the woes that were befalling this put-upon individual and how this might affect their ability to perform to the expectations I had set out at the beginning of the session.

I am not a nasty person, and generally I am sympathetic to people who have genuine difficulties. The problem was, having spent eight hours having to work hard to overcome the stream of negative comments output that she chipped in at every opportune moment to avoid the black cloud engulfing all the other participants, I just wanted to shake the energy sapper by the shoulders and shout "GET A PERSPECTIVE!" In the same group of participants was a lady who was in the middle of radiotherapy to combat cancer that was in all likelihood terminal. This participant, who had an incredibly sunny perspective and was, contributing positive, innovative, and creative ideas had decided to continue with the program because she wasn't going to let her life be determined by her illness and she was fed up of not living a normal life. This attitude is world beating. Nothing, other than death itself, will ever stop this lady from being everything she chooses to be because her attitude is that she can.

A Positive Attitude Is World Record Breaking

On 6th May 1954, Roger Bannister broke the four-minute mile barrier, running a mile in 3:59:40. Up to that point experts were saying it was physically impossible to run more than a quarter of a mile a minute. The theory was that if someone were to run faster than that, they would either break their femur or their brain would explode from the CO_2 build up. Today, given the athletic feats we witness, this attitude is really quite incredible and pretty daft. It is the epitome of the idea that you really don't know until you try. Eighteen months after Roger Bannister broke the four-minute mile barrier, 17 other people did the same. Attitude toward what appears to be possible is everything. When you choose an attitude of positivity, you have the energy and a natural striving mechanism that overcome the fear of failure. If you have an attitude that says all things are possible, then quite literally all things are possible. This isn't the same as having a false hope. Declaring I can fly and then jumping off a skyscraper without a wingsuit, that's just stupidity. No, having a positive attitude is about seeing the good things and having a perspective that seeks out opportunities. It is a positive attitude that makes the lemonade out of lemons.

Disney chooses to recruit its employees on attitude, because they believe that you can teach someone the skills required to a job, but it is hard to change attitude, and many practitioners in recruitment circles subscribe to this view. Research in social psychology shows that attitude is an important, distinctive, and indispensible concept, but attitudes are only relevant if they are considered alongside the social context or organizational environment in which they are being expressed. Fishbein and Ajzen (1975) sought to develop a theory of reasoned action and the theory of planned behavior; Fishbein and Ajzen (1991) argue that behavior was determined by a person's intention to engage in that behavior, and intention was determined by attitude, subjective norms, and perceived controls. Further research has established that both these theories provide reasonably good accounts of the relationship between attitude and behavior. However, when it comes to predicting behavior, then nothing can be taken for granted.

Attitude Is a Choice

Attitude is extremely important in how successful you are in your career. It is more important than the circumstances of your background, the qualifications you have, or your financial situation. In your career progression, it will be your attitude that will help you win promotions, more so than your skill and knowledge. You attitude will make or break your career and determine the future that you have. Your attitude has the potential to be one of the greatest strengths you have to play in being able to win the challenge and be instead of do.

But let's be clear—attitude is a choice. You can choose to be negative or you can choose to be positive. You can choose to think of yourself as a failure or choose to believe that it is possible for you to be successful. You can choose to view a situation as a problem or you can choose to view the same situation as a challenge, but an opportunity for you to shine. Attitude is something you can choose. Therefore, choose wisely. Are you going to be an energy sapper or a world-beater?

Manage Your Career Tool #14 – Ten Positive Things

The next time you find yourself in a situation that you find challenging or you feel negatively about, take a deep breath and list ten positive things about the situation. Once you have completed the exercise, read what you have written and meditate on it. Allow the positive elements of the situation become something that you believe are actually possible, as you do so notice how your attitude toward the situation begins to shift.

_____

_____

_____

_____

_____

_____

_____

_____

_____

_____

_____

_____

_____

CHAPTER 14

If at First You Don't Succeed

Flaming enthusiasm, backed up by horse sense and persistence, is the quality that most frequently makes for success.

— Dale Carnegie

Perseverance is an excellent quality to have, especially as an entrepreneur. Steve Jobs once said, "I'm convinced that about half of what separates the successful entrepreneurs from the non-successful ones is pure Perseverance". There is a saying that goes; if at first you don't succeed, try, try again. Another word for perseverance is Fortitude, which means having the strength to overcome obstacles to continue to perform. But very often, we can persevere in the wrong things. By this, I mean that keeping on trying something doesn't necessarily mean that what we are trying is the right thing to do. Maybe we should be trying something else. Perseverance doesn't mean continuing to do stuff that doesn't work, it just means continuing in the face of adversity.

Discipline and talent are important when it comes to succeeding in our careers. The concept of "The 10-year rule" suggests that those who are top in their fields will have spent ten years working full-time and being highly invested in their chosen practice. Bloom (1985) studied top scholars, students, and athletes and his research discovered them to not only possess talent, but also to be incredibly self-disciplined in their field of expertise. Research by Duckworth and Seligman (2005, 2006) discovered that it was self-discipline that mattered more than intelligence when it came to educational success and final grade achievements. Duckworth et al. (2007) also concluded that it was grit, and a dedicated pursuit of a long-term goal that was the only thing that separated talented people. They concluded that it was an individual's perseverance of effort, which develops the fortitude required to overcome obstacles or challenges in order to realize the achievement of the goal they pursued.

When to Persevere and When to Quit

It's hard to admit you have made a mistake. In fact, it is hard to recognize you have made a mistake; after all, no one sets off with the intention of doing the wrong thing. We all do the things that we think are right. It's just that, as we implement our plans, sometimes it turns out that what we thought was right isn't right after all. We've all heard the saying "If you keep doing the same thing, you'll always get the same results". So, what is it, give up or persevere? Personally, I think it means keep going, don't change your attitude, but change what you are doing. The other dilemma is when something was working, and then suddenly it isn't working anymore. However, sometimes you are doing the right thing, and it is a case of trying again and getting it right next time. But this then presents the challenge of us knowing what to try again, and what to not try again. We somehow have to develop an internal compass that indicates when you should adjust your approach and where should you plough on knowing that if you keep doing the right things it will succeed eventually. Since most of us don't all have a crystal ball to tell us whether what we are doing will deliver fruit in the future, we have to make a judgment call.

Evaluating Outcomes

Evaluation is an overused concept and an underused practice. But knowing what we need to continue with and what to discard comes from assessing outcomes and being honest in that assessment. My son has Dyslexic Dysgraphia, which means he struggles with visualizing words and, therefore, has to code every word he learns to spell. When he was younger, he was getting words from school to learn to spell, and every week I would test him, getting him to write the word he got wrong ten times, then tested him again. And every week, he aced his spelling tests. The issue was that he had succeeded in passing his spelling tests, but he hadn't learned how to spell, so once the test was over, the information leaked from his memory. The process of reading and writing has resulted in many false starts and we tried a number of different methods over the years. Eventually, having tried to teach him to succeed and failing, we turned to a professional and my son now attends additional literacy lessons with a specialist teacher. It seems to be working.

When it comes to something like reading and writing, the outcomes are easy to evaluate. Either you can, or you can't. For other things, measuring success is slightly more ethereal. But using the success measures that you developed in Manage your Career Tool #7, you can decide whether what you are doing is moving you toward that goal, or away from it. You can evaluate whether you should persevere with what you are doing and understand what needs to change, if success remains out of reach. Whatever the choices are that you make, it is important that you are disciplined in continuing to pursue your goal. They say insanity is to keep doing the same things and expecting different results. If your goal, your purpose, is worth pursuing, don't give up; persist in following the vision you have set yourself. Continue trying, but evaluate the outcome of you efforts. If the outcome of the action you have taken doesn't help you to move closer to your goal, then change what you are doing. It isn't about changing direction, it's about changing tactics.

Don't give up on dreams that are worthwhile, just give up on the stuff that isn't helping you get there!

Manage Your Career Tool #15 – Evaluation to Create Forward Movement

Giving up on an activity you are doing to get to the goal because it isn't working is different from giving up on the goal itself. If you evaluate the outcomes of your activity against your success measures and find that they are not helping you to achieve what you desire, then stop and plan your next move.

Below are some questions to help you evaluate where you are in achieving your success and help you create forward movement:

- What is taking shape?
- What is emerging from your actions and activities?
- What has challenged you?
- What is missing so far? What are you not seeing? What do you need more clarity about?
- What has been your major learning, insight, or discovery so far?
- What's the next level of thinking we need to do?
- What is the one thing that hasn't yet been said or done to reach the next level? What would that be?
- What would it take to create change in your current situation?
- What could happen that would enable you to achieve your success measure and feel fully engaged and energized about your situation?
- What's possible here and who cares?
- If your success was completely guaranteed what bold steps would you choose?
- What support do you need to take the next steps?
- What conversation, if begun today could create new possibilities for the future?

It is recommended that you make evaluation of outcomes part of your career-planning process. This means setting time aside at regular intervals (at least once every three months) to review progress, check outcomes, and decide what next steps need to be taken to move things forward.

CHAPTER 15

Surfing the Edge of Chaos

Chaos in the world brings uneasiness, but it also allows the opportunity for creativity and growth.

— Tom Barrett

Have you ever stopped to ask yourself why you do the things you do, and why you do the things you do the way you do them? It is a fact of life that human beings create order. Some like to create order more than others, and some individuals' sense of what order is makes more sense than others; but whatever degree of order we create, the fact is we have systems and processes in our lives that are a result of deeply ingrained assumptions or generalizations that influence how we understand the world and how we take action. These perspectives are also known as our Mental Models (also referred to in Chapters 9 and 10).

I once knew someone whose office and desk, to the untrained eye, looked like a burglar had come in and turned the place upside down; but if you were to ask that individual for a specific document or piece of information, they could find it instantly in a bewildering display of order in the chaos. For most of us, our everyday lives, even if they feel chaotic, are full of routines: the order in which you get dressed in the morning; the way you make your breakfast; how you tackle household chores; the way you stock your fridge. We bring our need for order into the workplace and start a whole series of routines: where we park our car; what we do when we get into the office; how we save our documents; how we file our paperwork; when we prefer to make phone calls; when we call meetings etc. But the problem with our routines and mental models is that they often clash with or get interrupted by someone else. For some, a break from the routine is a welcome distraction, for others, it disrupts their whole day and prevents them from being productive.

Balancing Complexity with Simple Routines

In a complex world, routines are essential to bring order so that things get done, and ensure that the things that need to get done, get done on time. Mental models help us make sense of the world around us. But routines and mental models also lull us into a false sense of security. They create a sense of having a handle on things and being in control. Worse still, they prevent us from thinking outside the boxes, systems, and processes that we have constructed. In a fast-paced world, routine prevents us from the dynamic and flexible thinking and ways of operating that will enable us to be proactive rather than reactive.

Mental models are often the greatest barriers to implementing new ideas in our life and work, and can lead us astray. Consider the story of the blind men and the elephant, where several blind men are feeling different parts of an elephant and describing it. The descriptions by themselves are inaccurate, but when combined into one, give a clearer albeit still flawed description of what an elephant really looks like. There does need to be a balance. Routines are important if they work, because routine can help us to be efficient. But organizational and personal effectiveness requires that we regularly commit ourselves to surfing the edge of chaos, forcing ourselves to challenge our mental models and ensuring we maintain a growth rather than fixed mindset.

Avoiding Liminality

A great analogy I heard recently is that of the rock pool, which helps develop the concept of living in a place of change and routine at the same time. First, imagine you are at the seaside. If you are lying on the beach or bobbing on the sea in a boat, you are in a place of routine, lulled into a sense of security, but you are in danger of being unprepared for changes that occur. In your own experience, you might have seen people on the beach caught out by a rising tide and have to hurriedly gather their belongings to stop them being swamped by the incoming waves. Or you may have seen individuals in a dinghy suddenly realize that they have drifted too far from shore, and struggle to bring themselves back to a safe place. The examples of the people on the beach being caught out by the incoming tide, or the people in the dinghy, can be analogous to an organization or individual being caught out by liminality. The term liminality is used to "refer to in-between situations and conditions that are characterized by the dislocation of established structures, the reversal of hierarchies, and uncertainty regarding the continuity of tradition and future outcomes" (Horvath et al., 2015).

But there is another place where you can place yourself at the seaside of organizational and personal effectiveness, the rock pool. Rock pools are particularly challenging and harsh environments. Plants and animals that live here must be able to cope with constantly changing conditions as water temperature, salinity, and oxygen levels fluctuate. Coping with all this and with crashing waves, in addition to avoiding predators, is no easy task. Yet rock pools are teeming with a rich variety of sea life that adapt and avoid liminality. Sea anemones, limpets, and seaweed are all stuck to rocks to prevent them from being washed away by the tidal currents. All can move from their anchored points when they need to, but they survive in the rock pool by being able to respond to the changing environment while maintaining a firm footing where they need to. This is the space that individuals and organizations need to establish to achieve effectiveness. They need to let go of the comfortable places and surf the edge of chaos, having a firm-enough grip on a solid foundation (purpose and values) while being flexible enough to respond to the changing requirements of a dynamic and fast-changing global environment.

Developing a Rock Pool Mentality

So how do you break out of your mental models and routines? You can develop a rock pool mentality by:

- Creating a safe environment in which people feel comfortable surfacing and examining their mental models; it must also be an environment where decisions are based on what's best for the individual or organization, not on politics;
- Helping people develop their skills of reflection and inquiry;
- Promoting diversity rather than conformity;

- Agree to disagree; everyone does not need to agree with the various mental models that exist; each one is just an additional piece of information;
- Getting comfortable with uncertainty; we will never know the complete story.

This process requires individuals and organizations alike to change how they think about the nature of work and life. Once those barriers are reduced, we can begin to see mental models becoming leverage points for the innovation and creativity required to surf the edge of chaos.

Manage Your Career Tool #16 – Breaking Mental Models

Adapted from Spodek (2013)

Changing mental models requires an examination of your beliefs and those things that you value and deciding whether those beliefs and values help you to achieve what you want to in life, or whether they are holding you back and preventing you from being a success. Once you have recognized any limiting beliefs and values, it is possible to begin work on renewing your mind and challenging your belief system in order to ensure that your mental model is aligned with your desired purpose. There are three stages to this process:

- Improving your awareness of current beliefs
- Deciding what mental models you do want
- Replacing beliefs

It is important that you realize that as you engage with these exercises that you understand that mental models don't always change overnight. Under pressure, it is easy to slip back into old ways of thinking, and you need to be determined to challenge yourself when you notice you are doing so, without being judgmental and beating yourself up for 'wrong thinking.' It is being deliberate in capturing thoughts that are unhelpful in pursuing your goal, and reiterating your new mental model until it becomes ingrained into your belief and value set.

Task 1 – Improving Your Awareness of Current Beliefs

This task is simply about taking notice of your beliefs and making a note of them. Over the course of one week, carry a notebook and pen with you. When you become aware that something in the environment is a trigger, take notice of the belief and write it in your notebook. No analysis is necessary at this stage, you simply want to capture a record of your mental life, the beliefs you have and the mental models you use to make sense of the world we live in.

_____

_____

_____

_____

_____

_____

_____

_____

_____

_____

_____

_____

_____

Task 2 – Deciding What Mental Models You Do Want

After you have completed Task 1, you need to spend some time deciding what beliefs and mental models are aligned with what you want in your life, and which of those are disabling you from achieving success and need to be discarded. For example; if one of your beliefs is "I am not good enough" and your mental model involves constantly feeling inadequate and having to strive to prove you are good enough, then this is not a life giving belief or model and would need to be replaced. Write down the beliefs and mental models that you want to discard below:

_____

_____

_____

_____

_____

_____

_____

_____

_____

_____

_____

_____

_____

Task 3 – Replacing Beliefs

Once you have decided what mental models you wish to discard, you will need to determine what you are going to replace them with. The beliefs that conflict with your goal need can only be challenged with something that works better for you. Using the unhelpful belief "I am not good enough" from Task 2, you would rewrite this belief as "I am good enough" and your mental model would be reframed as not needing to have to prove yourself to anyone. For each of the beliefs and mental models you highlighted in Task 2, write a corresponding replacement below:

_____

_____

_____

_____

_____

_____

_____

_____

_____

_____

_____

_____

_____

Conclusion – Are You Ready for Encounter

Here's to the crazy ones. The misfits. The rebels. The troublemakers. The round pegs in the square holes. The ones who see things differently. They're not fond of rules. And they have no respect for the status quo. You can quote them, disagree with them, glorify or vilify them. About the only thing you can't do is ignore them. Because they change things. They push the human race forward. And while some may see them as the crazy ones, we see genius. Because the people who are crazy enough to think they can change the world, are the ones who do.

—Apple Inc.

Do you feel it? I woke up this morning with a sense of purpose. Today is that day. It may seem like you have no idea what the day will bring, or that circumstances are muddled. You may not know what you are doing, or even why you are doing what you are doing. But maybe today is a day to set aside all the confusion, all the worry, and all the uncertainty and stand up and count today as the day that something new is going to happen. If you have completed all the Manage Your Career exercises and the associated tasks, you will have started you Challenge to Be and not to Do. As you begin to notice the changes and feel the difference that being rather than doing a job brings to your life, I encourage you to share your learning and revelation with others. Becoming an evangelist to set others free from merely doing a job to pursuing a life where you can pursue the release of your full potential.

Good luck and Best Wishes. I know you going to be awesome!

References

Adams, M.G., Schiller, M. and Cooperrider, D.L., 2004. With our questions we make the world. In *Constructive discourse and human organization* (pp. 105–124). Emerald Group Publishing Limited.

Apple Inc. Think Different, Advertising Campaign, 2006.

ASPS., 2016. New Statistics Reflect the Changing Face of Plastic Surgery American Society of Plastic Surgeons Releases Report Showing Shift in Procedures. https://www.plasticsurgery.org/news/press-releases/new-statistics-reflect -the-changing-face-of-plastic-surgery (accessed 31.05.2017).

Ajzen, I., 1991. The theory of planned behavior. *Organizational Behavior and Human Decision Processes, 50*(2), pp.179–211.

Berger, H., 1940. *Psyche*. Jena: Gustav Fischer.

Berger, W., 2014. *A more beautiful question: The power of inquiry to spark break-through ideas*. New York: Bloomsbury Publishing.

Bloom, B.S., 1985. Generalizations about talent development. *Developing talent in young people*. Ballantine Books, pp. 507–549.

Branson, R., 2011. *Screw business as usual*. London: Random House.

Buckingham, M., 2010. *Go put your strengths to work: 6 powerful steps to achieve outstanding performance*. New York: Simon and Schuster.

Byrne, D., 1961. Interpersonal attraction and attitude similarity. *Journal of Abnormal and Social Psychology, 62*(3), p. 713.

Clark, D., 2014. Your weakness may be your competitive advantage. *Harvard Business Review*. https://hbr.org/2014/02/your-weakness-may-be-your -competitive-advantage (accessed 01.06.2017).

de Waal, A., 1991. *Evil days: Thirty years of war and famine in Ethiopia*. New York & London: Human Rights Watch.

Deci, E.L., Koestner, R. and Ryan, R.M., 1999. A meta-analytic review of experiments examining the effects of extrinsic rewards on intrinsic motiva-tion. *Psychological Bulletin, 125*(6), pp. 627–668.

Dewey, J., 1933. *How we think: A restatement of the relation of reflective thinking to the education process*. Boston: D. C. Health

Duckworth, A.L. and Seligman, M.E., 2005. Self-discipline outdoes IQ in pre-dicting academic performance of adolescents. *Psychological Science, 16*(12), pp. 939–944.

Duckworth, A.L. and Seligman, M.E., 2006. Self-discipline gives girls the edge: Gender in self-discipline, grades, and achievement test scores. *Journal of educational psychology, 98*(1), p. 198.

Duckworth, A. L., Peterson, C., Matthews, M. D., and Kelly, D. R., 2007. Grit: Perseverance and passion for long-term goals. *Journal of Personality and Social Psychology, 92*(6), pp. 1087–1101.

Dweck, C.S., 2006. *Mindset: The new psychology of success.* New York: Random House Incorporated.

Fishbein, M., and Ajzen, I., 1975. *Belief, attitude, intention, and behaviour: an introduction to theory and research.* Reading: Addison-Wesley.

Gardener, H., 1983. *Frames of mind: The theory of multiple intelligence.* New York: Basic Books.

Gass, B., Gass, D. and Haliday, R.G., 2012. UCB Word for Today, Stoke on Trent: United Christian Broadcasters.

Grieson, J., 2017. Number of cosmetic surgery procedures in UK fell 40% in 2016. https://www.theguardian.com/lifeandstyle/2017/feb/13/number-cosmetic -surgery-procedures-uk-fell-2016 (accessed 31.05.2017).

Horvath, A., Thomassen, B. and Wydra, H. eds., 2015. *Breaking boundaries: Varieties of liminality.* New York: Berghahn Books.

Judge, T.A., Piccolo, R.F., Podsakoff, N.P., Shaw, J.C. and Rich, B.L., 2010. The relationship between pay and job satisfaction: A meta-analysis of the literature. *Journal of Vocational Behavior, 77*(2), pp. 157–167.

Losse, K., 2013. The return of the selfie. *The New Yorker,* 5.

Maslow, A.H., 1962. Some basic propositions of a growth and self-actualization psychology. *Perceiving, behaving, becoming: A new focus for education,* ed. A.W. Combs. Washington: Association for Supervision and Curriculum Development, pp. 34–49.

MacGregor, D., 1960. *The human side of enterprise* (Vol. 21, No. 166.1960). New York: McGraw-Hill.

Mezirow, J., 1990. How critical reflection triggers transformative learning. *Fostering critical reflection in adulthood,* ed., J. Mezirow. San Francisco: Jossey-Bass Publishers, p. 20.

Mercy Corps., 2017. Quick Facts: What you need to know about the Syria Crisis. https://www.mercycorps.org/articles/iraq-jordan-lebanon-syria-turkey/quick -facts-what-you-need-know-about-syria-crisis (accessed 31.05.2017).

Moon, J. A., 2004. *A handbook of reflective and experiential learning: Theory and practice.* Abingdon: Routledge Falmer.

NHS Digital., 2014. *Survey of Mental Health and Wellbeing.* http://content.digital .nhs.uk/catalogue/PUB21748 (accessed 31.05.2017).

Peter, L.J. and Hull, R., 1969. *The peter principle* (No. Book). London: Souvenir Press.

Peltier, J., Hay, A. and Drago, W., 2005. The reflective learning continuum: Reflecting on reflection. *Journal of Marketing Education,* 3, pp. 250–263.

Rawlinson, K., 2015. Shareholders receive too much money from business—Bank's chief economist. https://www.theguardian.com/business/2015/jul/25/shareholders-receive-too-much-money-from-business-says-chief-economist (accessed 31.05.2017).

Redman, M., 2006. *Beautiful news—Fearfully and wonderfully made.* London: EMI CMG.

Roth, P., 2012. An open letter to Wikipedia. *The New Yorker, 6.* http://www.new yorker.com/books/page-turner/an-open-letter-to-wikipedia (accessed 31. 05 .2017).

Satir, V., 1972. *People making.* Palo Alto: Science and Behaviour Books.

Schön, D. A., 1983. *The reflective practitioner: How professionals think in action.* New York: Basic Books. Inc.

Spodek, J., 2013. *ReModel: Create mental models to improve your life and lead simply and effectively.* SpodekAcademy.com.

Swannell, J., 1992. *The Oxford Modern English Dictionary.* Oxford: Clarendon Press.

Syed, M., 2010. *Bounce: The myth of talent and the power of practice.* London: HarperCollins.

Taylor, F.W., 1911. *Shop management.* New York: McGraw-Hill.

Trading Economics., 2017. Greece unemployment rate. https://tradingeconomics .com/greece/unemployment-rate (accessed 31.05.2017).

Wikipedia, Liminality. http://en.wikipedia.org/wiki/Liminality (accessed 15.11 .2012).

Woodward, C., 2015. *Winning!* Hachette UK.

Index

OTHER TITLES IN THE HUMAN RESOURCE MANAGEMENT AND ORGANIZATIONAL BEHAVIOR COLLECTION

- *Slow Down to Speed Up: Lead, Succeed, and Thrive in a 24/7 World* by Liz Bywater
- *The Illusion of Inclusion: Global Inclusion, Unconscious Bias, and the Bottom Line* by Helen Turnbull
- *On All Cylinders: The Entrepreneur's Handbook* by Ron Robinson
- *Employee LEAPS: Leveraging Engagement by Applying Positive Strategies* by Kevin E. Phillips
- *Making Human Resource Technology Decisions: A Strategic Perspective* by Janet H. Marler and Sandra L. Fisher
- *Feet to the Fire: How to Exemplify And Create The Accountability That CreatesGreat Companies* by Lorraine A. Moore
- *HR Analytics and Innovations in Workforce Planning* by Tony Miller
- *Deconstructing Management Maxims, Volume I: A Critical Examination of Conventional Business Wisdom* by Kevin Wayne
- *Deconstructing Management Maxims, Volume II: A Critical Examination of Conventional Business Wisdom* by Kevin Wayne
- *The Real Me: Find and Express Your Authentic Self* by Mark Eyre
- *Across the Spectrum: What Color Are You?* by Stephen Elkins-Jarrett
- *Life of a Lifetime: Inspiration for Creating Your Extraordinary Life* by Christoph Spiessens
- *The Facilitative Leader: Managing Performance Without Controlling People* by Steve Reilly
- *The Human Resource Professional's Guide to Change Management: Practical Tools and Techniques to Enact Meaningful and Lasting Organizational Change* by Melanie J. Peacock
- *Tough Calls: How to Move Beyond Indecision and Good Intentions* by Linda D. Henman
- *Human Resources as Business Partner: How to Maximize The Value and Financial Contribution of HR* by Tony Miller

Announcing the Business Expert Press Digital Library

Concise e-books business students need for classroom and research

This book can also be purchased in an e-book collection by your library as

- *a one-time purchase,*
- *that is owned forever,*
- *allows for simultaneous readers,*
- *has no restrictions on printing, and*
- *can be downloaded as PDFs from within the library community.*

Our digital library collections are a great solution to beat the rising cost of textbooks. E-books can be loaded into their course management systems or onto students' e-book readers.
The **Business Expert Press** digital libraries are very affordable, with no obligation to buy in future years. For more information, please visit **www.businessexpertpress.com/librarians**. To set up a trial in the United States, please email **sales@businessexpertpress.com**.

www.ingramcontent.com/pod-product-compliance
Lightning Source LLC
Chambersburg PA
CBHW050117210326
41519CB00015BA/3996